Tried and True

Tried and True

LESSONS, STRATEGIES, AND ACTIVITIES FOR TEACHING SECONDARY ENGLISH

Joseph C. (Joe) Antinarella *and* Ken Salbu

HEINEMANN
Portsmouth, NH

Heinemann
A division of Reed Elsevier Inc.
361 Hanover Street
Portsmouth, NH 03801–3912
www.heinemann.com

Offices and agents throughout the world

© 2003 by Joseph Antinarella and Kenneth Salbu

Library of Congress Cataloging-in-Publication Data
Antinarella, Joseph C., 1953–
    Tried and true : lessons, strategies, and activities for teaching secondary English / Joe Antinarella and Ken Salbu.
        p.   cm.
    Includes bibliographical references and index.
    ISBN 0-325-00474-9 (alk. paper)
    1. Language arts (Secondary).   I. Salbu, Ken.   II. Title.

    LB1631 .A56 2003
    428′0071′2—dc21   2002014465

Editor: James Strickland
Production service: Lisa S. Garboski
Production coordinator: Vicki Kasabian
Cover design: Jenny Jensen Greenleaf
Typesetter: Publishers' Design and Production Services, Inc.
Manufacturing: Steve Bernier

Printed in the United States of America on acid-free paper
07 06 05 04 03 RRD 1 2 3 4 5

To all the hardworking teachers
who love what they do and do what's right for their students

CONTENTS

PREFACE

Tried and True is a book for teachers and teachers-in-training containing approaches and activities for success, with samples and strategies borne of many years of diverse teaching experiences. We have taught thousands of students and teachers in dozens of courses from English 8 to graduate writing institutes, and in all cases our goal is to use and share methods that enable students to make meaning of what we present in our classrooms—simple methods that work.

We wrote this book for college students and student teachers, beginning teachers, and experienced teachers for practical, everyday use in their classrooms. While *Tried and True* will be most useful for English language arts teachers in grades 7–12, teachers of social studies, humanities, research, or writing courses will find the book useful as well.

Topics of our discussion include ones of interest to teachers and students of reading, writing, speaking, and listening across the disciplines. The book is laid out both topically and chronologically to parallel the school year. That is, the beginning chapters focus on topics germane to starting a teaching career or beginning the school year, such as reader response, classroom atmosphere, and planning effective lessons; the middle chapters address topics that interest teachers as the school year progresses, like managing workshop classrooms and planning interdisciplinary units; and the final chapters discuss end-of-the-year topics, such as creating final portfolio projects. Teachers are not bound to this chronology, however, in their reading and use of *Tried and True*: chapters are self-contained, and they need not be read or considered in strict sequence.

Tried and True features sample lessons, activities, and templates for teachers to use and adapt to their own classrooms. Each lesson or activity begins with a GTO statement:

> Grade or grade levels suggested for the activity
> Time required for the teacher and students to complete the activity
> Outcomes the teacher and students can expect from the activity

We offer student samples and responses to most of the activities we've included to help give readers a feel for the classrooms where the activities have succeeded—and for teachers to use as models or examples for their own students. As well, each chapter ends with an alternative activity, a method that might serve as a replacement for a classroom practice from which teachers need a reprieve.

A new teacher's challenges differ from those a veteran faces—but in all cases, being a successful teacher takes trial and error, practice and patience, reading and research, gut and intellect, heart and hard work. Teachers want useful, manageable strategies that engage students in learning. We take all this into account when we suggest the methods and activities that make up *Tried and True*.

Tried and True

1

Reader Response in
Today's Classroom

"Examine the parts, add them up, and see what they render."
—*Patrick Meanor*

One of the first ways a new teacher can jump into a successful classroom experience is by using reader response. Likewise, an experienced teacher looking for an approach to reading and literature can effect an academic, engaging classroom more easily through reader response than she can through study guides or discussion sessions that are not response-centered. Lessons built around too many recall or directed critical analysis questions can impede learning rather than facilitate it. Students need to share genuine connections to their reading—with respectful listeners—in order for an enjoyable reading experience and meaningful analysis to occur.

Reader response theory is grounded in reading as a transactional process, whereby a given literary work, and therefore its meaning, exists in the transaction between the reader and the text. No two readers will have the exact same reading experience with any given work. Each reader's experience with a text is influenced by many factors.

Using reader response as a theory that informs practice is a sensible way to approach teaching literature in the classroom; students' responses to the text are respected—and the teacher, through both choice and pace of readings that can elicit response and an open stance that encourages students to respond—becomes a fellow reader and questioner, one who knows how to facilitate learning as well as impart it.

While many teachers become experts at guiding students' reading, largely through carefully crafted questioning, successful teachers know that they cannot control every part of every lesson. Ironically, even the best teachers cannot order or predict with a high degree of accuracy or success what a student will learn or what will prompt that learning, understanding how students learn notwithstanding. Years of assemblies, music lessons, snow days and other absences, interruptions, and variables teach them that a "less prescription, more immersion" approach can be key in creating a classroom that works.

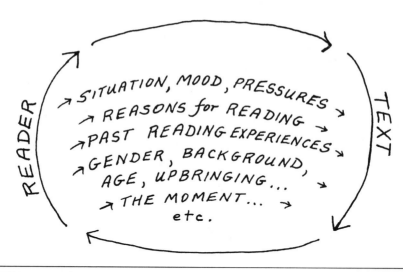

FIGURE 1–1 Reader text map

Students' involvement in their work is more important for their learning than the teacher's prescribed path. Learning is personal.

Using reader response is a simple and effective means to interact with and analyze literature in a classroom setting. It makes sense because

- The act of reading is unique for each reader, who brings selective attention and submerged associations to a dynamic and variable text
- Literature must have some connection to students' lives
- Students must discuss and question aspects of the text and seek valid answers: examine the parts, add them up, and see what they render

Response-centered critical theory, a fairly simple and sensible way to approach the study of literature, is nonetheless the subject of volumes' worth of a teacher's reading and study. For example, judging the validity of a student's response is just one aspect of reader response worth study in its own right. In most Methods of Teaching English classes, students study reader response—as informed in large part by Louise M. Rosenblatt—in order to examine issues inherent in reader response theory.

Our purpose in this chapter is to present some simple ways for teachers to help students respond to what they're reading, beginning with an informal survey appropriate for both new and experienced teachers.

Choosing Works for Classroom Study

Determining what (kind of) literature their classes will read and study, either as a whole class, in groups, or individually, is one of the first challenges new teachers take on, and it is an ongoing issue for veteran teachers. American schools are run by local and state governments, and they range tremendously in size, structure, curriculum, and quality. Some states have boards that approve textbooks for adoption statewide, perhaps limiting a teacher's choices to selections from books on that list. In some schools, teachers choose all works they present to their classes, making changes as they see fit; in others, teachers have little or no input. While their own involvement in selecting the number and types of works they will teach varies greatly from school system to school system, most teachers find ways to incorporate new or newfound readings into their lessons.

The following questions will help teachers assess the reading choices they make—and how they go about presenting those choices to their classes:

1. What determines the works that you teach during the course of a year? What are the selection criteria, and who applies them?
2. At your grade level (or, if you're not yet teaching, at, say, the ninth- or tenth-grade level), how many novels might you expect your students to read for class? How often do you plan for a novel? How long do you take to teach it?
3. Is biography/autobiography as important a genre as the novel? Should students read more biographies and other nonfiction genres? Do you apply different criteria to the selection and reading of these genres than you apply to novels?
4. How often do students read short works (in any genre, 1–3 pages) in your class? How do you use these works?
5. To what extent do the following issues play a role in your selection process: Reading level? Censorship? Multiculturalism? Gender bias?
6. Do you read critical analysis on a major work before discussing it? Do you expect students to read criticism?
7. Provide titles of three books you have read in the past year. To what extent are they books that you would consider teaching?
8. Give titles of three short works (again, any genre) that you feel would work well in eliciting student response.
9. Do you use study questions, study guides, reading-check quizzes, or unit tests to accompany students' reading? How/when are they

valuable? To what degree should questions integrate response with analysis?

10. How do you handle small group reading? Individualized reading?

There are no definitive answers to these questions. They might best be used as springboards for discussion or as a way for teachers to share successful approaches. For example, question 4 brings to mind the following "highlight and respond" method, which we used with Emerson's "Nature" (a two-page piece) as part of an interdisciplinary study on America's national parks.

Highlight and Respond

Grade: 7–12
Time: One class period (thirty to forty minutes)
Outcome: Critical reading and writing; sharing and synthesizing responses

This activity—and variations of it—can be used regularly in conjunction with short works of any type:

1. Read the piece aloud while students follow along.
2. When the reading is completed, ask students to highlight three phrases or sentences that "strike" them or "speak" to them. Give them a few minutes to do so.
3. Have students select one of the highlighted phrases and write it as a direct quote atop their papers. Students discuss the quote: paraphrase, tell why they chose the quote, what they find remarkable, etc. (free write—ten to twelve minutes).
4. Ask for volunteers (five or more) to share (read aloud) their chosen quotes and the related responses.
5. Ask students to comment upon and assess each other's responses: Which did they most enjoy listening to? Any surprises? Connections? Dichotomies?

"Highlight and respond" is a natural and effective way to have students engage with the text they're reading. The activity enables them to assess their own reading, thinking, and written responses in light of the body of their classmates' responses. It's an effective classroom management technique as well.

Writing Literary Letters: "Oh, Dicey, Do This . . . Oh, Dicey, Do That . . ."

Grade: 7–8; also useful for 9–12

Time: Ongoing, in class and at home; ten or fifteen minutes for a freely drafted letter

Outcome: Students develop voice and sense of audience when responding to literature

An effective way to use a reader response technique in the classroom is through the use of literary letters. Students write to the teacher (or to each other, perhaps as part of a cooperative group or a literary circle, or to literary pen pals, etc.) in response to their reading. We tried the approach for the first time with Cynthia Voigt's *Dicey's Song*; for the first time, we used no study guides or "Questions for Study and Discussion." Students said what they were wont to say, and, using a punch-and-bind machine, we published our writing in a class anthology entitled *Novel Responses*. Following are three samples:

> By far, *Dicey's Song* is the most boring book I've ever read in my whole entire life! No action at all. No real suspense, nothing! I hated it. It was all drama, nothing else, just drama: "Oh, Dicey, do this! Oh, Dicey, do that!" Talk about sickening things—this is the worst. It's the worst book to come along since *Julie of the Wolves*. But, hey. If you like boring drama and no action, *Dicey* is the book for you. Otherwise, if I were you, I wouldn't read this book if my life depended on it.
>
> Yours truly,
Donald

> *Dicey's Song*, a novel by Cynthia Voigt, is nothing to write home about. It was dull and boring. If the irritating characters weren't snorting, they were snapping or making mental notes. The book lacked many, many elements of entertainment. It had no action, romance, suspense, or even humor. Furthermore, the one time in the book someone died, I didn't even cry. *Dicey's Song* is one of the worst books I have ever read, and I would strongly urge you not to read it.
>
> Your friend,
Tony

"It had no action, romance, suspense, or even humor . . ." Tony was right. The book *did* have no action, romance, suspense, or even humor. And the characters were kind of irritating, snorting and snapping all the time, which made us examine our choice of books for whole-class instruction. We were forced to refigure why we had chosen the book, given what it lacked. What did the book have that made it appropriate for seventh graders in October?

Dicey's Song was a very interesting book. It shows many points of view and shows how the smallest amount of prejudice can ruin someone's life. I like the way Cynthia Voigt detailed and laid out the book. I also like the way she made me ask myself questions about the book. It was full of sharp turns and all-at-once dead stops. It gave me a new look at the world today and different feelings about beggars in the street, etc.

Signed,
Josh

Asking the Right Questions

Infusing a classroom with reader response does not mean the end of critical analysis, nor does it preclude the use of study questions for writing or discussion. There is, however, a distinct difference in the kind of questions a teacher asks when she wants to approach analysis through response. Many experienced teachers are masters at writing "old school" questions, manual-type questions reminiscent of the literature classes that many of us were trained in, three- and four-part questions written in "teacher prose," questions that accentuate a prescribed analysis at the expense of a real, visceral response.

Here's an example. As an exercise in reader response, we asked a student teacher to write four "Questions for Response" to Carol Bly's short story "Talk of Heroes," which we were using as part of an interdisciplinary unit on heroes and heroines. We would write four questions as well; we'd compare and assess the results, both with the student teacher and in that semester's Methods classes. Following are the two sets of questions:

SET 1: CAROL BLY—"TALK OF HEROES" POSSIBLE READER
RESPONSE QUESTIONS

1. Why is the character of Emily Anderson's daughter included in the story? What possible significance—reason—can you think of?
2. What point(s) is Emily Anderson trying to make with the Tusend Hjem audience? How does she get her point(s) across?
3. Upon returning home after addressing the Tusend Hjem group, has her attitude toward her daughter changed? (See p. 100.)
4. Is Willi Varig a hero? A drunkard or a has-been? Should we count his actions in the past—both "good" and "bad"—in assessing any possible heroic status?

SET 2: QUESTIONS FOR RESPONSE: "TALK OF HEROES" BY CAROL BLY

1. What were your impressions as you read the story?
2. How (specifically) does the story differ from others we've read this year?
3. Cite three instances or passages from the story where you see evidence of humor.
4. Talk about the heroes from "Talk of Heroes."

Here's how one graduate student responded to the questions, after he made clear his lack of interest—distaste, even—for the story:

> Personally, I hate the first set of questions—they remind me of the type of questions you find in high school anthology books. Nobody likes to answer these questions because most of the time they're so obvious that it feels like a waste of time to write the answers out on paper (such as questions 2 and 3). Questions 1 and 4 are thought provoking, but they seem like a chore to answer. In contrast, the second set of questions requires the student to know the same information but seems like much more fun because the student is in control. For example, question 4 from the second set is asking for the same information as question 4 from the first set. However, Question 4 from the second set allows the students to decide who the heroes are and why, instead of being limited to a specific line of thinking concerning Willi Varig. (The students will probably form similar questions and answers about Willi as a hero or a has-been on their own, anyway.)

Teachers should use questions as a part of whatever classroom configuration they choose; the type, quality, and teacher's execution of these questions determines, in part, how fully students respond. Keep these things in mind when choosing or composing questions for reader response:

- Write questions for response, not questions for analysis in the name of response (see Set 1, 1)
- Reader response questions are often simple in syntax but not in concept (see Set 2, 4)
- Reader response questions are open-ended, less teacher directed (compare questions 4)
- Reader response questions will elicit true, diverse responses rather than attempts to get the right answer (see Set 2, 3)

Keeping a Reader Response Journal

Grade: 7–12

Time: Ongoing, weekly entries

Outcome: Students have written records of their reading and responses throughout the year.

One effective way for teachers and students to keep an ongoing record of students' readings and responses, including responses to both individual choices and required reading, is to have them keep a reader response journal. This is simply a notebook where students are required to write at least (an average of) one thoughtful page per week in response to their reading. (*Tip for success:* a hardcover marble notebook works great for both traditional notes and responses to reading—notes are kept in the front half, responses in the back half.) It's not a place where they write in response to general prompts such as "My Most Embarrassing Moment" and the like. Rather, the journal accomplishes the following:

- Students keep track of their reading and reading growth
- Students' reading takes on an everyday importance
- Students can respond individually, and/or the teacher can direct responses and response times
- Students can share connections and opinions about their reading with others
- Teachers can assess the state, quality, and quantity of students' reading

Note the following two sets of response-centered questions for you to examine, use, or adapt, in journals or otherwise: One general set of questions meant to elicit response, and one set written specifically to serve as a final response to Richard Wright's *Black Boy*. The general set, "Reader Response Journal Entry," can be adapted for any grade level and taped to the inside of each student's journal for easy reference.

Reader Response Journal Entry

Write a response to reading selections as a way of exploring, making meaning, or preserving your thoughts and feelings. Use the suggestions below to guide you through your reflective journal entry.

1. **Quote** Choose a line, phrase, or word that you consider significant. Focus on noteworthy dialogue. Choose several lines in the piece if appropriate—discuss your selections. Make some connections and decisions about these quotations.

2. **Reactions and Impressions** Record these after your first reading. This can be in any form—free writing, notes, lists, stream of consciousness, etc. Reflect and comment on why you feel the way you do.

3. **Vocabulary** Highlight words that need interpretation, interest you, or that you feel are important. Highlight words that make you wonder. Consider these language highlights and give some of your thoughts about them.

4. **Questions** Pose a few thoughtful questions about the reading—questions that require analysis, definition, or clarification. What questions do you need answers to immediately? Are there unresolved questions? What are your answers?

5. **Smart Remarks** Make some honest comments about the subject, characters, actions, events, or connections the piece suggests. These might be criticisms or "compliments" of the writer or the behavior of the characters or the style of writing. Do your remarks reveal something that you might discuss further? Why are you bothered, satisfied, or moved by what you've read?

6. **Just Some Good Writing** Record an example of powerful writing—something brilliant, shocking, confusing, etc. Why might your selection qualify as a "golden line" worth remembering? What more can you say?

Topics for Reader Response: Black Boy

Directions: Respond to _____ questions/topics. Write freely, honestly. Respond in paragraphs. Use pen if you write by hand.

A. "Each Negro is a little bit white, and every white is a little bit Negro . . . Both are caught in a common human predicament. Each needs the other." —Kenneth Clark, *Dark Ghetto*

B. "Blues belong to the black man. No white man can sing the blues and really know what he's talking about." —Ray Charles

C. "When you starts measuring somebody, measure him right, child, measure him right. Make sure you done taken into account what hills and valleys he come through before he got to wherever he is." — Lorraine Hansberry, *A Raisin in the Sun*

D. What has reading *Black Boy* taught you? What new awarenesses have you experienced as a result of reading the book?

E. Which scene from the autobiography did you find most amusing? Most touching? Most gratifying? Most shocking? Most disturbing?

F. What are your thoughts about Richard's struggle to become a writer? How do Richard's experiences relate to your experiences as a writer/ feelings as a writer?

G. Why is Richard Wright's *Black Boy* worthwhile to read?

H. I wrote a letter to an African American editor for a local newspaper, asking for some advice for us (as a predominantly white class) to consider when dealing with or examining race relations. Here is part of what he said: "If I can humbly pass on but one or two concepts that have seemed to register with white students, it is simply this—to challenge themselves to ignore for a moment the bizarre images of movies, newspapers, and TV." What "bizarre images" do you suppose the editor is challenging you to ignore? Ultimately, what do you suppose he means?

I. When Richard graduates from the ninth grade, he refuses to deliver the speech that the principal has written for him and insists on using his own. Neither speech is reproduced in *Black Boy*. Write your version of either Richard's speech or the principal's speech.

J. When he was living and working in Memphis, Richard discovered the writings of H. L. Mencken. How did reading then become an even greater passion for Richard?

K. Discuss how your reading of *Black Boy* has enabled you to understand the effects of racism and/or understand human reactions to racism.

Varied Approaches for Teaching Poetry: Response and Analysis

In the reading and teaching of poetry, both response and analysis are integral, whether they coexist comfortably or stand at odds. In either case, analysis through response is one natural way for teachers and students to approach poetry, for responses emanate from the composite of students' experiences, including previous knowledge, questioning, and speculation.

The chart that follows is a valuable resource for teachers of any grade level who want simple but effective ways to present poetry to their students.

1. READ and LEAVE
   Do not discuss
   Let the poem "say everything"

2. TWO QUESTIONS ONLY
   Do you like it?
   Why?

3. WHAT and HOW
   What does the poem say?
   How does it say it?

4. UNIQUENESS
   How does this poem differ from
   others read thus far?

5. PRY WITH WHY
   Why did the author write it?
   Why did s/he choose this form?

6. UNIVERSALITY
   Is there an important one?
   Discuss "personal" universalities

7. RELEVANCE
   Does the poem relate to life today?

8. SOME ONLY'S
   Deal only with mood
   Deal only with sound
   Meter and rhyme, from,
   figures of speech, etc.

9. MAJOR APPEAL
   Is it chiefly to the intellect?
   The senses? Emotions?
   What combination?

10. MAJOR METAPHOR
    Is there one governing the poem?

11. JOURNALISTIC QUESTIONS
    Who is speaking? To whom?
    What is the occasion? When, where?
    How do form and technique help?

12. STRUCTURAL STEPS
    What happens in the first stanza?
    The second? Where do significant
    changes come?

13. PAIRED POEMS for comparison

14. PAIRED PUPILS for explications
    One: Structural analysis/basic form
    Two: Meaning through images,
    sounds, allusions, etc.

15. GROUP PRESENTATIONS
    Each group presents a different poet
    Each student reads and presents a
    poem by the author

16. SILENT TREATMENT
    (Pass the Chalk)
    Put statement or question on board
    Hand chalk to a student

17. PERSONAL PROJECTION
    Tell what you think a minister,
    parent, principal, sibling would
    think of the poem and why

18. THREE-STEP ANALYSIS
    (difficult poem)
    Explication (difficult words)
    Penetration (structure and
    technique)
    Speculation (extended meanings)

19. BOIL IT DOWN
    Write the "message" in no more
    than twenty words

20. TAPE RECORDER/VIDEOTAPE
    Different students record stanzas of
    a long poem; two students present
    a dialog poem; solo performance
    with music

FIGURE 1–2. Varied approaches for teaching poetry

It makes poetry accessible to both. The chart is useful for a brief lesson or prompt using a short poem at the beginning of class (Approaches 1, 2, 10, or 16 would work here). For example, a teacher might use 10, Major Metaphor, in presenting Langston Hughes' "Mother to Son."

Likewise, the chart provides frameworks for presenting longer poems or projects: Structural Steps (12) and Three-Step Analysis (18) work well in teaching challenging poems like "The Raven," where students want to know what's happening, what it means, and all about the atmosphere. Major Appeal (9) could be part of a very successful approach to teaching Shakespearean sonnets. The possibilities are endless.

Finally, this chapter offers an alternative to the standard essay or paragraph response—for when students need to write, but not necessarily in expository prose.

Alternative Activity: Writing Acrostic Poems

Grade: 7–9; also useful for 10–12
Time: One class period
Outcome: Writing about literature (or any other content area/topic)

Instead of asking a specific or academic question, or instead of giving an essay test, have students write an acrostic poem, based on literature or on any other topic. They will be writing and thinking, and you will be pleasantly surprised at the results. Here's an example using Mildred Taylor's novel *Roll of Thunder, Hear My Cry*:

Directions: Write the title of the book vertically down your left margin, and write an acrostic poem in response to the novel. Aim to capture in words what you deem remarkable or essential about the book.

Roll of thunder
O hear my cry
Lord of waters
Light the sky

Ol' white man wants to take our land and
Family's pride away

Time will come
Hurts all will be healed, but
Until that blessed day
Nothing will stop us from fighting for freedom
Don't nobody stop us from fighting for freedom
Even though the night men ride in darkness,
Ride to sink us down, to lower us,

Hear us now, see us now
Eye us with hatred
And we, in the end, will
Ride out triumphant

My mother and father, and
    those before them,
    stand behind me now
You, roll of thunder

Child of heaven
Ruler of all above and
    below,
You, listen in my time of
    despairing,
        Oh roll of thunder
            Let my people go

—Alesandra Bellos

FIGURE 1–3. "Roll of Thunder, Hear My Cry" poem

2
Classroom Environment
"This Ain't No Good Place"

"I don' like this place, George. This ain't no good place.
I wanna get outa here."
—*John Steinbeck*

Even in the lush Salinas River Valley of California, Lennie in *Of Mice and Men* intuitively felt that he was in a mean place where he could not flourish or, perhaps, would be unable to survive. Lennie's perception and ability to articulate it, likewise, rings true in many schools and classrooms. This underscores a feeling that a classroom is uninviting. It suggests an atmosphere consciously or unconsciously created by teachers: one that can inhibit students from taking risks, from becoming active learners or from working in ways that are productive. This is apparent in a classroom in which the following conditions exist: students generally feel incapable, are insecure about how to proceed, or ask too many prescriptive questions about instructions. They hesitate to make a move, to strike out on their own.

In another environment, students are not overly concerned about minutiae or a list of do's and don'ts. They focus on the work, and their feeling is positive. Creating an inviting environment, a "good place" conducive to learning, should be a primary concern of teachers. It's good practice to attend to classroom atmosphere—to create one that allows the best work to be done. Similarly, teachers set the predominant tone in a classroom, one that will produce a necessary visceral reaction in students, either drawing them in or discouraging them. Creating this secure, communal atmosphere is fundamental to drawing students in. Effective learning, despite technology's impact on education practice, still can be enhanced by a communal condition that makes gathering in a classroom unique, and it's one crucial factor that teachers can manipulate. Attend to atmosphere first and students respond.

Knowing this or being reminded of it causes us to make critical decisions before attempting to deliver any curriculum to students. We've got to confront students' perceptions of school, our subject, and learning, and then, if necessary, establish a more positive working environment. In his book *How*

Children Fail (1995), former Boston schoolteacher John Holt identifies teacher behaviors that affect learning:

> We encourage children to act stupidly, not only by scaring and confusing them, but by boring them, by filling up their days with dull, repetitive tasks that make little or no claim on their attention or demands on their intellect. Our hearts leap for joy at the sight of a roomful of children all slogging away at some imposed task, and we are all the more pleased and satisfied if someone tells us that the children don't really like what they are doing. We tell ourselves that this drudgery, this endless busy work, is good preparation for life, and we fear that without it children would be hard to control.

Unfortunately, Holt's ideas about the classroom, written more than twenty-five years ago, are prevalent today; they color our own notions about what's best for kids. At the same time Holt wrote these words, our well-intentioned high school English teacher ran her class through declamation exercises. These strained oral performances required each of us to stand before our classmates and our evaluator to recite memorized passages of literature. She kept her eyes and ears trained on us—her head erect, her posture perfect, she sat with pad on lap listening, ready to pounce on any mistake we might utter. Our voices took on an expressionless, flat quality as each student struggled to remember or raced through lines that had little meaning. On these days, like Lennie, we, too, felt an abiding dread. We internalized a feeling about the classroom as a "bad" place.

We must question everything we do in the classroom that affects the way students feel. Are we cementing long-lasting feelings about classrooms as places to avoid or as inviting places? Holt's words reflect the reality of too many school experiences then and now. (Exercises like these still occur in American schools.) And while many students survive, unbearable routine or unnecessary discomfort or intolerable drudgery do not serve the best interests of the student community. We should continually consider our lessons:

- Do they develop skills that students can apply elsewhere?
- Do they give students experiences and practice to learn independently?
- Do they ultimately prepare students to continue to learn?

The answers to these questions should guide us, as reflective teachers, in designing lessons that create the "right" environment. This chapter shows ways to establish a positive atmosphere in a classroom, without which students cannot reach their potential.

Opening the Door

One way to establish an open atmosphere is to design a personal survey to begin work with a new group of students. A survey gets students writing about themselves; it allows them to tell their own stories. Some teachers begin a new class with a lot of teacher-talk—reviewing rules, going over procedures, and giving instructions. Students generally play a passive role in this transaction. Beginning with a *Writing Needs Assessment* (Figure 2–1) or a *Literature Survey* (Figure 2–2) in an English class gets students involved immediately.

There are important reasons why you should create a personalized survey for your class:

- The information you receive quickly helps you to know your students.
- The assignment shows that you value a student's history.

Name _____ Date _____

Complete this survey honestly and as completely as you can. I'll use it to help guide the direction of this class. Be specific.

1. My most memorable writing experience . . .

2. I hope this class will give me . . .

3. A characteristic of good writing I often notice is . . .

4. Writing is . . .

5. I am comfortable writing when . . .

6. In writing, I need to work on . . .

7. My academic goal is . . .

8. I often write about . . .

9. The *best* thing about writing is . . .

10. On the back of this form, write a brief narrative of who you are. What should I know about you to help you be successful in this class?

FIGURE 2–1. Writing Needs Assessment

- The feedback helps you to engage students on personal levels.
- You gain useful background information.
- The responses suggest a starting point for teaching—a way to proceed based on what students know.

Completing the statements in the Writing Needs Assessment eases students into writing.

The Literature Survey asks students to tell about their experience with literature. The responses to this survey help us make critical decisions about teaching and forge personal connections with students.

Personal surveys generate useful information more than provide definitive answers. The objective is to learn about our students and their feelings related to our subject. Our response to these surveys, either informal or formal, and our subsequent behavior become critical to creating a dynamic atmosphere where more risks are encouraged and taken, rather than a prescriptive

For the purpose of the questions below, consider anything under the heading of literature. Use an attached separate sheet of paper if necessary.

1. What have you read that has impressed you?

2. What type of films do you like (adventure, comedy, action, thriller, etc.)?

3. What do you read regularly?

4. What is your favorite type of literature? Your least favorite?

5. List any extracurricular activities or hobbies you enjoy.

6. What has caused or could cause you not to like literature?

7. What is the best piece of literature you can remember reading? Explain briefly.

8. What plays have you seen and enjoyed?

9. What are your academic goals?

10. Please write a little about yourself. (Include anything I should know to help you be successful in this class.)

FIGURE 2–2. Literature Survey

one in which students conform to minimal standards. Simply put: this first writing assignment is worth reading, worth talking about, and worth using. There's no better way to begin teaching.

In a prophetic tone, John Holt emphasizes a key point in his book when he reveals that, "It is not the subject matter that makes some learning more valuable than others, but the spirit in which it is done." The lack of "spirit" is the primary reason why too many students are uninspired in classrooms, disinterested in learning, and resistant to opportunities. Beginning with personal expressive writing assignments paves the way for open communication and creates essential common ground; it allows the "spirit" of each student in the class to emerge.

Likewise, it makes sense for teachers to design assignments in which students have choices and can write about familiar subjects for which they have a passion. Omitting this step may allow teachers to present course material sooner, but we gain insights and develop trust using this approach that makes teaching content, in the long run, more meaningful and effective. Consider writing an open letter to students and parents to make this connection. Distribute it and invite reaction in writing. Respond to the reactions you receive in class and discuss the issues that arise.

Here's a sample of one of these communiqués that might be shared:

OPEN LETTER FROM YOUR TEACHER

The aim of this class is to use the most recent research on writing and the writing process so that you can practice and enhance your writing. You will write five to six original pieces from which you will choose three to submit for a grade near the end of the course; you should keep all drafts and "chunks" in your working portfolio. I will postpone grading these drafts until they are in the most final form acceptable to you and are submitted in a presentation portfolio. You must share your writing with others and consider suggestions that may result in revisions so that you can produce your best possible work. In these ways, we can establish a working community of writers.

What kind of writing will we do in this class? It should be writing that will expand your thoughts and feelings; it should interest your audience as well. Above all, the writing should be honest, thoughtful, and worth reading. Let the following ideas guide you:

1. Write with authority about specific events, places, feelings, and people you know.
2. Use specific examples to make the writing real.
3. Have a personal investment in what you write.
4. Take some risks.

Many of the pieces you write will deal with personal topics; write about what you know best and share your experience and thoughts. You should understand that a good piece evolves as you "work" it. Prepare to read aloud, rework, tear apart, polish, fine-tune, ask for feedback, or re-arrange a piece until you get it the way you want it. You'll find "your way" to writing the best pieces only after scrutiny and reflection. Try to see writing through new eyes; be open to new perspectives and changes in the way you generate and revise pieces. All this will help you take ownership of your writing. In order to gain power over your writing, you'll need to concentrate your effort.

Often questions arise from the open letter. Our taking time to address these questions gives students and parents a good feeling about a teacher and builds a sense of community. Additionally, an open letter works well at the end of the year as a way to convey some final thoughts. Tailored to reflect the personality of each class, the letter is a nice way to close out the class.

Stepping Out: Negotiating the Curriculum

A lot has been written about designing effective lessons to include the right components to ensure motivation, attention, and retention. Teaching methods textbooks provide model lessons and outlines to follow emphasizing these three important attributes. Classroom experience teaches us that effective lessons depend, too, on student-generated questions, comments, and thoughts—their active participation—more than a rigid adherence to a master plan. Design activities to ensure that students play an active role. Interaction motivates them, keeps their attention, and helps them to retain what they've learned.

We know that movement alone in a classroom—*plowing* through work or *covering* curriculum—is not enough. We know that following "the plan" sometimes doesn't work. We may remember many hours, as beginning teachers, spent writing linear lesson plans aimed at reaching a definite goal. We remember, too, the specific moment during a lesson when panic set in, when a student unexpectedly revealed the answer that ended the lesson before its time. What did we do? With the evolution destroyed and the rhythm interrupted, we began to backpedal, to review, to fill in with something until the bell rang. This is no surprise. We believed in and relied on scripted lessons. And many times we wrote the scripts as we went along. After one of these experiences, we may have felt that the classroom was not a "good place."

An occurrence like this does not need to destroy a lesson or ruin the classroom experience. On the contrary, reacting to unexpected discoveries during lessons—actually encouraging them and "working off" them when they do come—should define an environment we want. While there is some insecurity in leaving the script, the possible discoveries are worth it. We're not suggesting that teachers operate without a plan; we're emphasizing the need to be alert to possibilities that occur only during a "live" performance, that are often unscripted. These teachable moments engage students. Here is a Top 10 list with suggestions that can take you beyond what you might plan:

TOP 10 WAYS TO DESIGN LESSONS THAT REACH STUDENTS

10. 'Vary the avoidance. (Don't let the daily routine grind students into complacency.)

9. 'Answer questions with questions. (Learn to ask the "right" open-ended questions.)

8. 'Get everyone to play. (Keep the playing field even by getting students to join in.)

7. 'Work the class, don't let them work you. (Work *off* your students, not *on* them.)

6. 'Listen to what students say. (Tune in with an ear that hears more than what's said.)

5. 'Be alert for the unexpected! (Be ready for what's lurking, what's about to be discovered.)

4. 'Know your material. (Learn to roll with it, connect it, apply it.)

3. 'Lead the class. (Don't dictate, overcontrol, overmanipulate.)

2. 'Keep moving but change the pace accordingly. (Allow necessary digressions.)

1. 'Provoke, promote, cajole, counsel, suggest, challenge. (Then, get out of the way.)

These suggestions help us to choose and adapt activities to fit our styles of teaching and the way our students learn. These general precepts allow us the flexibility to use, discard, or modify our "original plan" as the lesson takes shape. We should apply these to the specific needs of our students.

What Do You Mean, "What Does It Mean?"

How do we "challenge, then get out of the way"? We've all heard one question students ask that supersedes others in a lesson: "What does this mean?" It's a concrete question and fundamental to understanding. If we want students to think critically, to solve problems, to become independent learners, we need to decide if we will answer this question. We start by letting students make meaning of a text or problem, but, at times, we give in to frustration or time constraints and just tell students "what it means." We often respond to another prevalent question that students ask: "What do you want us to do?" Similarly, it's easier to say what we want and not prolong the mystery. There are several reasons why students raise these questions:

- We've conditioned them to focus on prescriptive details.
- They know we expect the right answer.
- We penalize wrong answers.
- We eventually tell them the answer we "wanted."

The barrage of questions comes when students, lacking confidence, are challenged or when a definitive answer is not immediately clear. We've taught students to rely too much on us for answers. If we want independent learners, problem solvers, and critical thinkers, we need to foster these roles. We can achieve this by designing activities that require students to think and, in the process, give them confidence to trust their thoughts.

An *Anticipation Guide*, used as a prereading and as a postreading activity, inspires independent problem solving that we want students to demonstrate. One objective of an anticipation or prediction activity is to prepare students to receive and process whatever follows—a reading, a film, an exercise, a performance, or a presentation. Readiness or lack of it affects students' ability to make meaning. Anticipation guides provide a framework for students that will promote thinking and generate discussion.

The statements in the sample *Anticipation Guide*, for use with Seaborn Jones' poem "The Red Horse," create the following conditions:

- Disclose preconceived notions students may have.
- Create constructive tension.
- Allow students to make application to the reading.
- Lead students to see a change in their thinking.
- Make students commit.

"The Red Horse" works particularly well because its theme reinforces the idea that we are all capable of interpreting literary works. The poem urges everyone to find personal meaning. It shatters the belief that writers intentionally hide their meaning. To reinforce this idea, show several Chagall prints or ask students to find samples on the Internet (type "Marc Chagall" into any search engine to find online images). Students should see Chagall's works so they can use their imaginations to make meaning of the paintings. This kind of assistance in any lesson adds the necessary component to make the application real for students.

First, students should individually complete the "Before" column of the anticipation guide based on their feelings or their general knowledge. Poll the class to determine any trends that students indicate by their answers. An informal statistical analysis using a rough percentage works well; record these on the board to help students visually see the results. Read the poem aloud. Without any discussion, ask students to complete the "After" column based only on what the poem suggests. After working through these three stages, students should discuss their choices to clearly differentiate between their own thoughts prior to reading and their answers based on the text of the poem. Focus on particular statements for which there is some controversy or change in feeling.

An *Anticipation Guide* and "The Red Horse" poem follow.

Grade: 9–12
Time: One class session
Outcome: An introduction to appreciating/understanding poetry

"The Red Horse" Anticipation Guide

Before you read Seaborn Jones' poem "The Red Horse," decide whether you agree (A) or disagree (D) with the statements below. Share your answers before reading the poem with your group or the class. *After* reading the poem, respond to the statements based only on the reading. What change in thinking is interesting to discuss or write about?

BEFORE / AFTER

____ ____   1. Art conveys a meaning intended by the artist.

____ ____   2. Art can be understood by everyone.

____ ____   3. Interpreting poetry requires experience more than intelligence.

____ ____   4. Readers should search for hidden meaning in a poem.

____ ____   5. Written or verbal miscommunication is a universal experience.

____ ____   6. It's frustrating when people don't understand what you mean.

____ ____   7. We make meaning by comparing the unknown to what we know.

____ ____   8. Maybe there's a way to tell time by peacock feathers.

THE RED HORSE

When the woman in the museum
looked at the Chagall, she said,
"But what does it mean?

I don't like art where the artist hides the meaning."

Flying fish, man with goat's head
offering a bouquet of fireworks
to an upside down bride.

Once I was pulled over by the police;
I had laryngitis and all I could do
was make a sound like a cross between
a goose and a fog-horn.

When I tried to write a note
explaining my condition, I realized
I couldn't spell laryngitis
and handed them a piece of paper that said,
"I have Larry."

They passed it back and forth
saying, "What does he mean;
what does it mean?"

Maybe I should have handed them
a drawing of a violinist with no head.
Or like the clerk in the store
when I asked the time, responded,
"I don't know; I'm just hired help."
Then presented me with a peacock feather.

What does it mean?

Maybe there's a way to tell time
by peacock feathers. Something buried
in the mythology of hired help.
Circle of children
pointing feathers toward the moon.

I feel about the woman in the museum
the way she feels about Chagall:
what does she mean
what does he mean?

The peacock spreads his fan of fireworks.

It is time.

Seaborn Jones

An anticipation guide shows students that they can make meaning by comparing their original ideas to another set of ideas gained by reading. It's good practice to tap what students know or think—their prior knowledge or opinions—before introducing new information. The threat of giving a wrong answer is diminished in this process; the challenge to find new ideas, to change thinking, or to discover a new perspective becomes the focus. An anticipation guide will encourage students to examine text more closely and see nuances of meaning. They gain confidence in their ability to think for themselves.

Tip for success. Break down elaborate or difficult reading selections to focus on several key concepts. Decide on these and compose statements to cover an appropriate range of reading interpretations and connections, from concrete to abstract. You'll find that your statements may need revision as you test them in practice. Good statements give rise to lively discussion; let that be your guide in writing them. These statements become natural prompts for journal writing or more formal essay writing.

Beyond Journal Writing

Journals, in a variety of forms, should allow students to clarify their ideas, to see what they think. Unfortunately they have been often misrepresented or misused. Encourage and expect students to use journal writing to think and reflect, so they gain a necessary independence in their writing. Students need to see the value in recording their thoughts—even if disjointed at first. Journals make students commit their thoughts on paper—ones they know and ones that unknowingly emerge when they begin to write. We should present a journal as a valuable thinking/writing tool, initially and then upon reflection of what was originally written. If we want students to use what they've written in their journals as a way to expand their thinking beyond the initial writing, we've got to plan journal extension activities to provide this opportunity.

Here's a sample student activity that will achieve this thought expansion:

Grade: 7–12
Time: One class session
Outcome: Seeing value in using a journal to promote further writing and thought

Reader Response Journal—Extension Piece
This activity requires several actions:

- Read over several of your journal entries.
- Choose one or more and reflect on what you wrote.

- Highlight the original writing in your journal.
- Then, write beyond what already exists.

It's that simple. Plan to write at least a one-page extension in any form you wish. Use these ideas to guide your extension:

- What more can you say about the idea(s) you've written about?
- What feeling do you detect in your initial writing?
- What can you add to clarify or apply your meaning?
- In what ways do you still feel the same about what you initially wrote, or in what ways have you changed your mind?

Here's a sample student entry and extension:

ORIGINAL JOURNAL ENTRY

In the pasture behind my grandmother's farm, a creek, surrounded by banks of mud and silt, tall trees, and massive rocks uncovered by erosion, works its way through her land. Often animals gathered there to drink. My cousin and I spent hours upon hours down by this creek just being kids. We played on the banks, searched for snakes and went swimming in the one spot where the water was chest high.

Going to the creek was the one thing I missed most about home when it became time for me to go. I made up my mind about life sitting by that creek. The days of spending time walking down by the creek with my cousin are gone. It has been seven years since we went to the muddy creek. He lost the meaning of his life to trouble and drugs. Now when I am at the farm, I spend my time by the creek alone listening to nature.

JOURNAL EXTENSION

My first entry about the creek on my grandmother's land was mostly of a description of a place and how I felt when I went there—our original assignment. I can see now that the connection to my cousin was strong. Maybe the piece was more about him than the creek? I'm not sure. I picked up an attitude of regret about leaving this place and time in my life. I probably should write about that more. I went back to the creek recently, so I thought I'd write about my feelings then. Here's my extension:

The Creek

Those summers in Tennessee, down by the creek behind my grandmother's farm, are vivid in my memory. The creek, always the place I went to think about my life and what I wanted to do, has not lost its magic. I returned there recently, and it had the same effect on me.

The massive roots of old oak trees, uncovered over time by erosion, line the banks of the creek. Rocks peek through the water, enough to walk on to pass safely across the creek. I can still spot snake holes, deer and fox tracks leading up to the water. An occasional bird feather floats down stream.

Sitting astride an oak tree that had fallen across the creek, I relaxed and listened to the leaves blowing in the wind. I remembered my cousin, who has stopped going down to the creek with me, and wondered what happened. He changed during the school year that I went to South Carolina. I'm not sure a trip to the creek can help him anymore.

This sample extension shows what can happen when students reconsider what they've written and determine whether they have more to write. Encourage students to begin writing in response to the questions we pose, and then move naturally into writing more about some idea that emerges because of this self-reflection. Give students the opportunity to write about what they've written and the chance to explain what they've done and what they want to do. This dialogue (written or verbal) leads to better writing. This excerpt shows a student continuing his thought and revealing a memory that evokes feelings that he can rediscover and explore. This activity, if used at various intervals during the year, convinces students that their journals are useful to them in the writing process. It promotes more frequent journal writing and more expansive follow-up journal entries. Ultimately, the journals take on greater use and importance.

Extending the Classroom

Design lessons for discovery to keep students actively involved. Consider a class-to-class distance-learning project, a meeting of minds through the mail. More than a literary pen pal exchange, a shared project like this is worthwhile for a variety of reasons:

- It supports the need for students to see their learning go beyond their own classrooms.
- It promotes tolerance, understanding, and genuine sharing of ideas.
- It gives students some control over their learning.
- It encourages improvisation, invention, and cooperation among students.

Before email or live video broadcasting from classrooms was a reality, we designed this project to bring two groups together by mail. With technology available to students and in schools, the methods and speed for exchanging information have increased. Our initial idea was to exchange and compare student essays based on our reading of the same novel. We began there. The evolution of the project moved us into areas we had not envisioned.

We started the project by exchanging student-generated surveys, personal letters, examples of local artifacts, and classroom videotapes. We thought, at first, that eleventh graders in a Virginia high school and eighth graders in a Long Island middle school might not be interested in exchanging their writing. We thought that the mix might not work. The spirit in which we presented and conducted the project eliminated this concern for the most part. We downplayed the age difference. The defining identities emerged naturally, when one class became representatives of the rural South, and the other class became northern urban cousins. Our first writing lesson emerged: the need to dispel stereotypes. This lesson also applied dramatically to Richard Wright's *Black Boy*—the novel we chose to read.

We allowed for the necessary superficial student exchanges—important to establish their identities—and reveled in the more serious exchange of ideas provoked by varying interpretations of the book. More than just differences of opinion, we noted that each group expected misunderstanding or misinterpretation based on age or experience or regional influences. Again, we were driven to design lessons that allowed our students to discuss these real issues. *Black Boy* or any book with narrative appeal and controversy can provoke students to say or write what they really think, especially when they are afforded the anonymity and security of distance. Our expectations, uncertainties, and convictions gave us chances for some real exploration and testing beyond the confines of our individual classrooms. The student-to-student exchange became the defining element that transcended any superficial obstacles. Kids writing to kids made the difference.

Critical Thinking and Writing: Using Cutouts

Responding to cutouts emerged as one of the most successful and notable activities we used in our class-to-class project. The activity helps define ideas, feelings, and biases students harbor about what they read. Each class collaborated in small groups to create pasteup sheets of words and phrases—cut out of magazines—that connected to the novel. The connections ranged from literal and specific to abstract and interpretive. Students wrote personal commentaries to explain their choices and included these with each cutout sheet. Selecting word and phrase cutouts, writing about them, and reviewing other responses urged students to think deeply about the novel and to think critically about their ideas. When each group reviewed and discussed the other's selections, students were engaged even more.

Figures 2–3 and 2–4 show some sample student cutout sheets we exchanged.

Grade: 7–12
Time: Two class sessions
Outcome: Students think critically and write reflectively

Here are several student responses based on a sample cutout sheet we exchanged between the two groups:

> "Daily bread"—Like racism, hunger was a major factor in Richard's life. It's not the hunger we feel when dinner is an hour late, but more of an aching hunger.

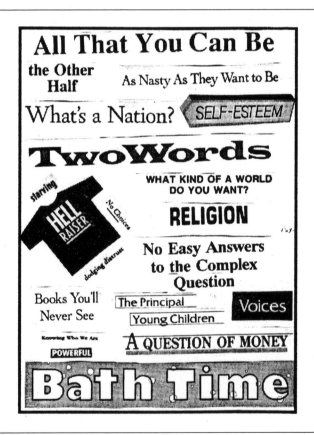

FIGURE 2–3. Cutout sheet 1 from *Black Boy*

"A house is not a home"—When Richard's mother got sick, he was sent to live with his relatives. This moving from house to house became a routine for Richard. He always had a house to live in, but none of these were his home.

"In the city of fear"—If you were black and living in the South, you always had to watch your back. Living in fear of attack or harm must cause serious personal problems.

"Sometimes the best way to stand out is to blend in"—In the library incident, Richard had to decide whether to play along with being discriminated against or speak up. He decided to play the game, so he could check out books and read what he needed to read to educate himself. He made a good choice.

The personal and expressive quality of these responses makes them significant. Students reveal a deep understanding that go beyond what textbook prompts can generate. As an alternative to a steady diet of teacher-generated question-and-answer assignments, cut-outs offer a refreshing change. The visual presentation appeals to students, and they react favorably to the freedom to choose what to write about and how to answer. We found the following benefits in using cutouts:

- Students think and write critically.
- Students naturally progress from concrete to abstract interpretations.
- All students can participate on many cognitive levels.
- Possibilities for divergent thought are increased.
- Students see language and words as having meaningful connections.

Beyond this project, cutout sheets related to any topic or area of study can motivate students to produce insightful writing. Keeping them on file to use with future classes or sharing them with other teachers makes the effort worthwhile and communal.

Figure 2–4 shows an additional sample cutout sheet we generated related to a specific work of literature.

Grade: 9–12
Time: One class session
Outcome: A multilevel interaction with literature

Here are several useful adaptations:

- Have students bring in several cutouts for a homework assignment—they can attach their written responses.

smoke...
smoke...   Let's work together and   **enemies**   FULL OF GOOD IDEAS

THE 'CREATURE'

KNOW-IT-ALL   A forest fire is no picnic.

rivalry   security   **Rules**   The Rock.

A SKY-HIGH DOGFIGHT

MOB SCENE   **MEMORIES OF DEATH**   I did things I shudder to think about."   Hair

SIGNS OF WEAKNESS ABOUND

on the beach   water?

PLAYING   Who will lead ?   **OUT OF THE DARK.**

meat   Under Pressure

"HALT, WHO GOES THERE?"   **THEM'S FIGHTIN' WORDS!**

large shadows   **PLOTTING FOR SUCCESS**   He's a peach of a guy,

WANT TO SUCCEED, NOT JUST SURVIVE.   *Cut the work*   MASTERMIND

CAUGHT

The Solution   **BETWEEN ROCK AND A HARD PLACE**

The bonfire      **HAS EVOLUTION BROUGHT US TO THIS?**

the way it happened   Notice the big smile on his face?

The Dark **get so irritating**

FRUIT   **Starting over**

A new way of seeing things.   **THE BRINK OF DEATH,**

the enjoyment that goes on and on.

FIGURE 2–4. Cutout sheet from *Lord of the Flies*

- Create a class mural or bulletin board of collected cutouts centered on a character, concept, or unit of study.
- Use several cutouts as a section on a test to elicit original responses.
- Collect cutouts related to a lesson or topic and distribute one to each student as a journal prompt at the beginning of class.

- Have collaborative groups of students create cutout journals with a particular focus (a single character, a specific setting, a singular concept).
- Use a cutout sheet as a prereading activity—a type of anticipation guide.
- Use a cutout sheet as a review before a test on a unit or piece of literature.
- Display cutouts that have elicited interesting or contradictory responses.
- Create a file of general topic cutouts on 3 × 5 cards to use as writing prompts.

This mutual activity helped us see the value in using words and phrases cut out of magazines; it encouraged students to think and write in ways that many textbook questions could not. Beyond this revelation, we saw how cutouts turned much of the responsibility for making meaning over to students, engaging them on levels that positively affected the classroom environment.

Alternative Activity: Letters from the Heart

Grade: 7–12
Time: One class session
Outcome: Opening lines of communication between students and the teacher

Letters from the Heart is a useful alternative to the writing regimen; it's a low-tech activity that fosters a communal atmosphere by allowing students to share necessary thoughts. Students take a break from routine assignments to write a letter to the teacher. The purpose of the letter is simple: students write what's on their minds and what they need to say—sort of a "state-of-the-student address." Letters from the Heart has several benefits:

- It validates writing as a communication tool.
- Students write about what's working and what's not.
- All students have a direct link to the teacher.
- Students can share in writing what they won't say.
- We can make adjustments based on students' comments.

Are students honest? Do they write what's expected? Mainly, yes. Writing "from the heart" establishes an informality that students like, yet the written form maintains some formality in the exchange. Whether students write what they truly feel or what they think we want to hear, it's valuable for us to read what students tell us, and it's important for us to address these comments.

Ideally, teachers like students to be internally motivated. In practice, we must create situations and an environment so that students can make decisions and assume responsibility for personal choices. These experiences motivate many students and empower them to make learning personal.

In *Schools That Work* (1993), George H. Wood encourages teachers to develop "enticing and exciting classroom activities and a genuine commitment to the classroom as a community." He goes on to say that "the creation of this environment is woven into the very fiber of the class experience; everything teachers do works to foster the sort of self-discipline necessary to make communal life possible." We can create an atmosphere where self-motivation and self-discipline flourish. Enthusiasm, cohesion, cooperation, and renewed spirit are results of a thriving classroom community. It's crucial for learning.

3
Planning Effective Lessons

"I liked working in this class. The work wasn't easy,
but it was never overwhelming."
—Joe Milazzo

Experienced teachers know—and new teachers quickly discover—that planning and executing lessons is a complex process fraught with irony and devoid of guarantee.

How many times have we thought

- The lesson would work, but it failed
- The lesson would fail, but it worked
- We had made ourselves clear, but we hadn't
- Our plan would take a full period, but it took ten minutes
- A task would take ten minutes, but it took a whole period
- The students had mastered a given skill, but they hadn't
- The students needed help with a given skill, but they didn't
- We'd be in the mood to watch skits, but we weren't
- The kids would be interested, but not really
- We'd seen everything, but we hadn't

Of course, teachers need to be flexible in designing and modifying their lessons, but the foundation for any lesson is the atmosphere and functioning of the classroom itself. A setting where the teacher shows a clear sense of purpose and a keen awareness of student involvement will lend itself to successful lessons.

Many forces drive a teacher's lessons, including and beyond the teacher: home and family; in-service training, graduate courses, and seminars; time and behavior management; routines and procedures; rules and expectations; successes and problems; testing and measurement; and student response. As well, lesson planning takes on many configurations, and it encompasses everything from a simple mini-lesson (discussed in some detail in Chapter 5) to an interdisciplinary unit plan (see Chapter 7) to the yearly syllabus or curriculum that may be in effect in any given school, county, state, or other educational jurisdiction.

In short, lesson planning is a primary focus for teachers, its implications essential and its parameters broad. While teachers need many resources to help them prepare their lessons, the following hints, structures, and sample lessons should be helpful.

The Lesson Plan Book

Many school systems require teachers to write daily lessons in a plan book, collected or checked weekly or monthly by a chairperson or supervisor. These books encapsulate plans into boxes wherein the teacher lists and briefly explains the topics, aims, procedure, and homework for each class, with arrows and crossouts indicating needed changes. Teachers' experiences with and need for plan books are as varied as the teachers themselves, but mapping out plans is almost always useful. Note the example in Figure 3–1 of how a week's plans might be written.

Note that each day's plans are an outline of what could be written into a formal lesson plan. Three classes begin with minilessons: Monday and Thursday's lessons set the stage for that day's workshop class, and Wednesday's minilesson on *Irony* is a follow-up to the day before. On Tuesday and Friday, the teacher conducts whole class lessons (a short story each day), beginning with an introduction—or, as Friday's plans show, an anticipatory set of questions.

A valuable note here: effective teachers use many different models and methods in their lessons, rarely limiting themselves to any one way. They take some leads from James Britton, for example, but they also use the work of James Moffett, Lev Vygotsky, Nancie Atwell, and others whose philosophy makes sense to them or whose approaches have proven successful.

The following structures and samples may be helpful to teachers and teacher educators who need to write formal lesson plans.

Writing a Formal Lesson Plan

Student teachers often wonder whether or not cooperating teachers write plans (like the ones they're required to write) for their own lessons. When cooperating teachers reveal that they rarely write such plans, student teachers often question the value of such plans. The value is this: writing a formal lesson plan requires that a teacher carefully consider all facets of a lesson and put those facets into cogent writing. This process helps to transform thinking into practice and practice into a guiding philosophy. New teachers must

LESSON PLANS *K. Salbu* FOR THE WEEK BEGINNING _10/20/98_

GRADE 8 . ROOM	GRADE ROOM	GRADE ROOM
SUBJECT *English*	SUBJECT	SUBJECT

10/20 MONDAY

<u>Reading / Writing Workshop</u>
1. Mini-lesson: Workshop choices and logistics
2. Individual workshop pursuits: write/revise reports; free writing; read book of choice; response journal entries; try something new.
3. <u>Homework</u>: Reports due tomorrow; reading & response

10/21 TUESDAY

<u>Short Story: "Charles" by Shirley Jackson</u>
1. Introduce and read story aloud.
2. Reader response
3. Notes: Foreshadowing and Irony
4. <u>Homework</u>: Read and respond to the books of your choice.

10/22 WEDNESDAY

<u>Reading / Writing Workshop</u>
1. Mini-lesson: Irony in "Charles"
2. Individual Workshop Pursuits
3. <u>Homework</u>: Reading and Response; Notebooks/Journals are due next week.

10/23 THURSDAY

<u>Reading / Writing Workshop</u>
1. Mini-lesson: Using free writing and writing folders.
2. Individual Workshop Pursuits
3. <u>Homework</u>: Reading and Response

10/24 FRIDAY

<u>Short Story: "The Parachutist" by</u>
<u>D'Arcy Niland</u>
1. Anticipatory Set
2. Read story aloud
3. Complete open-book comprehension test
4. <u>Homework</u>: Reading and response; notebooks/journals due next week.

MEETINGS and APPOINTMENTS THIS WEEK:

FIGURE 3–1. Lesson plan page

know that inherent in a successful veteran's unwritten plan are all the elements called for in the written plan—it's just that practice and experience can eventually minimize the need for a formal structure.

A formal lesson plan should be titled and can be divided into these five parts: materials, approximate length of lesson, aim/statement of purpose, procedure, and assessment.

Materials. List what you and the students need for class, perhaps including who is responsible for bringing or providing them. Consider the efficacy (availability, age-appropriateness, placement, probable effectiveness, etc.) of the materials you choose. Know where all the materials on your list are and how and when you plan to use them.

Approximate length of lesson. Not all lessons are one class session in length, and those that can be accomplished in one session may well connect to the previous or following lesson. In a sentence or two, identify the length and scope of your lesson. Give your lesson direction and connection. (Samples of all lesson parts follow in this chapter.)

Aim/statement of purpose. Although this section of the plan is the third of five parts, it is the foundation—the reason—for all other parts. For new teachers especially, the aims (or objectives) of a lesson can be difficult to figure out, let alone state. A good way to start is to consider just three points:

1. State your aims in active terms (action verbs, active voice) of what students will do. When teachers first ask Methods students to draft aims, they are inclined to write, "First, I'll do this and then I'll do that . . ." forgetting that the aim of the lesson is for the students. We know that teachers are concerned about delivering their lessons, but both the lesson plan and its delivery will be clearer when students are the subjects. Note the deliberate and active voice in these aims: "Each student will write a poem . . ." and "Students will analyze and assess . . ."

2. Include both primary and secondary aims. In other words, write aims that address both what students will do and why they will do it. The "what" is the secondary aim—or vehicle—for the primary aim of the lesson: the "why."

This simple anecdote illustrates the concept. Recently in school, our students were seated in groups of four, writing and illustrating "keepsake" poems (Sample Lesson 1). A colleague of ours peeked in and quipped, "I know what you're doing, but what are you saying you're doing?" We laughed because we immediately identified her implication: "I know what you're doing—coloring!—and what you're doing is not enough!" With one comment, she illuminated a key concept: you can't just say what students are physically doing—because "what" they're doing can seem simplistic or somehow inappropriate without the "why." She was warning us, "You'd better have a good reason for these kids coloring, other than you don't feel like lecturing anymore!" She was right—and in terms of illustrating "keepsake" poems, the illustrating is the vehicle, or secondary aim, for the primary aim of the lesson: "Students will analyze and assess how single objects from their own lives speak about the meanings of those lives—past, present, and future."

Here's another example: An eleventh-grade class is reading aloud Act I, scene i of *Macbeth*. The principal passes by, hears the witches, stops in, and says, "Sounds interesting—what's on the agenda today?" and the teacher or a student replies, "We're reading *Macbeth*." A perfectly acceptable response here is certainly not adequate for when that same principal asks the teacher for a written lesson plan, including aims, prior to an observation.

The written plan would be better expressed like this:

- Students will read aloud Act I, scene i of *Macbeth*. (What you're doing.)
- Students will examine the presence and roles of the witches in the scene. (What you're saying you're doing—a primary aim, focus, or reason for the lesson.)

3. Address thinking skills beyond recall. Almost all lessons should aim for more than recall of factual knowledge; students need to use acquired knowledge and comprehension in order to analyze, synthesize, and evaluate information.

Teacher training courses often present lists of words and phrases for teachers to use in designing a lesson's aims and procedures; and they have an endless variety of titles, like "Model Questions and Key Words to Use in Developing Questions" and "Expanding Brainpower." Most often such models are attributed to the work of Dr. Benjamin Bloom and identified as "Bloom's Taxonomy." They are divided into six levels of cognition: knowledge, comprehension, application, analysis, synthesis, and evaluation. Simply put, these levels go from the simplest cognition (knowledge) to the most complex (evaluation). For students to analyze, create, and evaluate information, they must show knowledge and understanding as foundations.

Here are some prompts to help teachers incorporate these levels of cognition into the aims of their lesson plans:

- Knowledge: Students will name, state, list, label, define, describe, identify.
- Comprehension: Students will outline, summarize, explain, translate, paraphrase, show similarities and differences, interpret.
- Application: Students will predict, demonstrate, show how, tell what will happen, solve, illustrate, construct.
- Analysis: Students will examine parts of the whole in order to classify, differentiate, compare/contrast, hypothesize, clarify, draw conclusions.
- Synthesis: Students will create, plan, design, develop, originate, formulate.
- Evaluation: Students will assess, judge, appraise, critique, debate, determine.

Procedure. Step by step, state what the teacher and students will do during the course of the lesson—from start to finish. Be thorough but not exhaustive—perhaps five to eight steps. Include procedures of classroom maintenance, wherever appropriate, as well as academic procedures. Include notes, questions, and examples as part of the procedure (if they're brief) or as a separate entity (if they are lengthy).

Assessment. In a brief list or paragraph, tell how you and students will make final judgments about the lesson and its success; methods might include a simple culminating activity for discussion, writing, or sharing; display of a project; or a reflective journal entry.

The sample lesson plan that follows uses the structure outlined and discussed above. It is the kind of lesson plan teachers often write—an adaptation of an idea or plan that the teacher has read about and would like to try. In this case, our plan is based upon a suggestion we discovered in *The Story in History: Writing Your Way into the American Experience* by Margot Fortunato Galt.

Sample Lesson Plan 1: Writing Keepsake Poems
  Grade: 7–12
  Time: One period and follow-up (note details in lesson plan that follows)
  Outcome: Students write poems for display alongside keepsakes

Materials. Assorted paper; pens (colored pencils, crayons, etc.); copies of books and/or poetry "connected" to the assignment: for example, Cynthia Rylant's *Appalachia* (1993). Each student should bring to school the object (or a sketch, photo, etc.) he has chosen as a keepsake.

Approximate length of lesson. One forty-minute period, to be followed by continued writing, revision, editing, drawing, and preparation of final manuscripts, in class (during workshop) or at home.

Aim/statement of purpose. Each student will write a poem describing/telling about a keepsake (artifact, heirloom, or memento) that has personal or family meaning. Students will engage in the writing process from brainstorming to preparing a final manuscript. Students will provide illustrations, photographs, or actual keepsakes for display alongside their poems. Students will analyze and assess how single objects from their own lives speak about the meanings of their lives—past, present, and future.

Procedure. (*Note:* This lesson depends upon reading and discussion as foundation and your success in getting a good number of students to bring a keepsake to class.)

1. Introduce the lesson with a recap or sharing of a related piece of literature.
2. Tell students to clear their desks except for paper, pen, and keepsake.
3. Have students answer these questions about the objects they've chosen (questions should be on chalkboard, easel, or handout):
    *   What is it?
    *   How old is it, and how do you know its age?
    *   Who gave it to you?
    *   What has the item endured?
    *   What memories does it evoke in you?

Allow sharing and discussion while students complete this task.

4. Ask students to examine the objects themselves and continue writing. Have students use any of the following prompts they choose:
    *   Look at the object, and notice what your eyes see first. Describe that detail.
    *   Write a list of details and random memories.
    *   Weave together information and description with memories.
5. Close the lesson by having students informally share (within groups if they're so arranged for the lesson, or as a whole class) what they've written or by addressing the class' progress and direction in a brief wrap-up.

Tip for success. The procedure of this lesson involves students in the first steps of the process of writing a keepsake poem. During subsequent classes and at home, students will work the words, ideas, and images from the lesson—adding and deleting as they revise into a poem (free verse).

Assessment. Display students' writing, photographs, illustrations, and keepsakes in an appropriate school location (keepsakes should be safely displayed in a locked showcase if actual items are used). If the lesson is part of an interdisciplinary unit or project, assess the discoveries of the lesson in light of the larger project.

This lesson can be adapted for use in many different classes on different grade levels, and it inspires students to connect and respond to important aspects of their lives through poetry.

The lesson works best when the teacher gives time and attention to both process and product; students need time to write and revise their poems, and their work must be shared. Note these:

DOG TAGS

Travels through battle,
on the chests and
in the pockets of the men
to whom they belong.

Like collars for animals,
they identify the dead
when lost—
forgotten is the unknown.

Just shiny tin pests
that return without owners,
they always survive.
But to those who return,
they are forever lucky charms.

Kristen DeFontes

CHARLIE'S CHAIN

This is too simple—
There is nothing to describe:
it's just a chain,
Charlie's silver chain
This is the easiest part.
Everything else is hard
When it comes to Charlie's silver chain.
He wore it every day.

It clanked against his neck when he chased a car
or when he fetched his ball.
It was often hidden by his black and white fur.
Sometimes a ribbon would show.
It's more than just a chain.
It's full of memories both good and sad.
Someday, with a new dog,
when the time is right,
I will place this chain on his neck,
hoping that he will be as good and as loyal
a friend as Charlie was.

Michael Fox

Sample Lesson Plan 2: "Me . . . Then and Now"
   Grade: 9–12 (also useful at the end of grade 8)
   Time: 3 to 5 class periods, not necessarily consecutive
   Outcome: Students free write, create a Venn diagram of adjectives and
   adjective phrases, and write compositions of comparison/contrast.

Like the previous lesson, this one can be adapted for many different subjects
and grades; however, because it involves students assessing and writing about
their own growth and change, it might be more effectively used during the
second semester of a school year. Unlike the previous sample, this lesson is an
original one, and it is not written into a formal lesson plan. Instead, it is organized into three segments, all of which can be accomplished primarily in
school: free writing, creating a Venn diagram of adjectives and adjective
phrases, and a composition assignment. The first two activities might be considered prewriting activities meant to engage students into thinking processes
and organizations that will help them to accomplish the main task: writing a
composition of comparison/contrast.

Free writing. Ask students to write freely for ten or twelve minutes (see
Chapter 5 for more on free writing) on any topic(s) that might link their
thinking to both the past and present. You might simply write on the board,
"Write freely for ten or twelve minutes about the past and/or the present."
Or, you might give the students a few specific prompts:

   • Write about a favorite toy you had as a child. What made you so
     fond of it/why did you like it so much?
   • What living person would you most like to meet and talk to? Why?
     What would you ask or say?
   • Describe your first (or any other) vivid childhood memory.

- If you could go back in time, where and when in your life would you go?

Tip for success: You need not forewarn students of their ultimate writing assignment before you ask them to free write. Allow them to approach the task as a worthy one in itself. As well, resist the urge to answer students' questions about this (or any other) free writing assignment; insist that they just write. If your classroom is an arena for a chorus of questions like, "Does it have to be a famous person?" or "Do we have to write about the past *and* the present?" the "free" loses its impact and the atmosphere might not lend itself to thoughtful writing.

Creating a Venn diagram. As a precursor to this assignment, we gave students a minilesson and a skills sheet on adjectives and adverbs. We based the mini-lesson on the simple and helpful chart shown in Figure 3–2.

Here are directions you can give your students for the Venn diagram segment of the lesson: Compile a list of words (adjectives and adjective phrases) that describe you as a child. Compile a second list that describes you as you are now. Compile a third list that describes you always. Then, create (draw) a Venn diagram that depicts you then, now, and always.

In addition to dictionaries and thesauruses, we had stacks of new and old vocabulary workbooks for students to peruse in search of words. As well, we

FIGURE 3–2. Adjective–adverb chart

explained what a Venn diagram is and put a model and simple example on the chalkboard. (See Figure 3–3.)

Students listed their words on scrap paper or wrote right onto rough Venn sketches. Before they began final work on white drawing paper, we showed students samples of already finished diagrams, not all of which used the traditional intersecting circles. But dependence on models or samples can inhibit originality, so we showed students models only briefly before putting them away. Alongside their writing, the finished products make for an interesting display.

Following is the third segment of the lesson, the composition assignment. We designed it in the same format students would see on a standardized writing test later in the year. Use the assignment as written, or modify it to suit your needs.

Composition Assignment. Me . . . Then and Now

Directions: Write a composition based on the situation described below. Read all the information carefully before you start to write.

The situation: You are in some ways a different person now than you were five (or more) years ago; you indicated these similarities and differences in a Venn diagram of adjectives and adjective phrases.

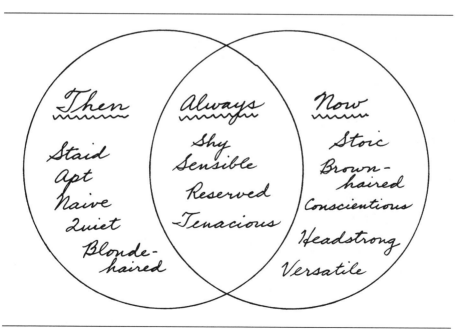

FIGURE 3–3. Venn diagram

Your task: Write a multiparagraph composition of approximately 300 words (you may write more) describing yourself by comparing what you were like five (or so) years ago with what you are like now. Explain how you feel about your growth and change. Be sure to accomplish the following in your composition:

- Compare the new you with the old you by describing similarities and differences
- Provide enough specific details about yourself to make the similarities and differences believable and clear
- Explain how you feel about the changes in you
- Organize what you write

SAMPLE METHOD OF ORGANIZATION:

Paragraph 1: Introduce yourself—write an inviting lead
Paragraph 2: Discuss similarities in the old you and the new you
Paragraph 3: Identify and discuss specific differences between the old you and the new you
Paragraph 4: Conclude by discussing how you feel about the new you.

Write ~ Revise ~ Proofread/Edit ~ Prepare a Proper Final Manuscript

One more note: Instead of requiring each student to use the same structure for writing a paper of comparison/contrast, we include a sample method of organization for students to use if they choose to. Because writing doesn't necessarily occur in the fashion shown by the sample method, it's important for students to engage in their writing freely before they ascribe this structure (or any other) to it.

Comparison/contrast papers can be difficult for students to write, especially if they attempt to follow a given structure too early in the writing process. First, to keep their words and voices honest, we suggest that students write freely. Then, they can organize their ideas and regroup. Often, their content will suggest an effective structure.

Teaching Skills Lessons

Despite college and graduate school experiences, we enter our profession not really knowing all the skills we need to know or teach. What formal grammar should seventh graders study? Eleventh graders? At what grade level should students read unabridged Dickens, and what are they meant to get from it? Isn't what constitutes reading and literature far broader than what many secondary school curriculums assume? How and when do students learn research writing skills? Who decides?

When we first plan lessons to teach whatever skills our local school or state requires as curriculum—if any—we discover that we need to know more. We do our homework and teach those skills in isolation, often without a full understanding of the topic or why we're teaching it: the seventh-grade teacher teaches participles, gerunds, and infinitives, but can't explain why; the tenth-grade teacher teaches Dickens, but doesn't know what specific skills might foster a successful reading experience: Do students need processing skills in order to understand what they read? Can they use a terminology appropriate for writing a character analysis? Can they differentiate between plot and theme?

An important thing to know is this: what teachers experience in the process of learning and teaching their subject material over the years shapes and improves their craft. A promising new teacher who has a tough time knowing what grammar to teach and how to teach it, for example, will search for information and turn that search into a learning experience for everyone. Both teacher and student learn simultaneously. Experienced teachers who finally understand the intricacies of the grammar they have been teaching for years can now present difficult concepts to their students in simple, effective ways.

Most teachers will use a variety of methods and materials in order to teach required skills or ones they deem necessary. We think it will be helpful for teachers to consider the following hierarchy of skills acquisition, keeping in mind that learning occurs on each level.

Demonstration. The teacher demonstrates a skill or rule, using a textbook, notes, handout, chalkboard examples, etc., and students demonstrate use or mastery of that same skill. The skill is not taught or learned as an integrated lesson—it is what we think of as "naked" or "isolated" demonstration. For example, to help prepare them for achievement tests, a ninth-grade English class studies Solving Analogies for three days, even though the topic does not directly relate to the reading or writing that makes up the bulk of their curriculum study.

Integration (immersion). Often, content will suggest an effective structure. This is why successful English teachers like to integrate skills instruction with whatever content areas they're studying in class. The content of their lessons will help determine which skills the students might have to learn/review in order to succeed at the lessons. Here are two examples of integrating skills instruction with content:

- In a class where students are writing explanatory pieces, the teacher might present a minilesson on how to indicate and punctuate sequence in their writing (see Chapter 5 for additional information).
- If students are having difficulty reading and understanding short stories or passing comprehension quizzes, or where reader responses have not demonstrated enough insight, the teacher might give a lesson on the process of reading: decoding, using context clues, using prior knowledge, making predictions, drawing conclusions, self-questioning, noting contradictions, monitoring comprehension, searching for answers, etc.

Speculation. Sometimes English language arts teachers (and texts) aim for student mastery of given skills in simple contexts; but if students become too comfortable in showing such mastery, they stop thinking and learning.

As students demonstrate given skills in given contexts, the teacher should set them off balance again, perhaps asking a "what if" question that relates the skill as learned to the skill in a larger setting. Or, a student himself wonders about applying the skill in a different way.

Note these two examples of "what if" questions:

- Is the word *however* always followed by a comma?
- Does a semicolon always precede *however* in the middle of a sentence?

Suppose students learned to follow the word *however* with a comma when it begins a sentence (However, the joke was on us.) or when it connects the two main clauses of a compound sentence with a semicolon (We didn't expect to like the movie; however, we really enjoyed it.). The teacher then might pose the above questions for speculation.

Interpretation (interpolation). Students and teacher now have the opportunity to add to their learning, to insert new rules, structures, or meanings, to make further connections. The teacher who has posed the two new *however* questions determines when and how to answer those questions with the demonstration of new structures and whatever explanations or further questions are fitting. For example, the teacher could use the two questions themselves as examples of sentences where *however*, because it is used as a noun rather than a conjunctive adverb, needs no further punctuation:

Question: Is the word *however* always followed by a comma?
Answer: In neither the preceding question nor in this sentence does a comma follow *however*.

Question: Does a semicolon always precede *however* in the middle of a sentence?
Answer: No, it does not; however, in this sentence it does.

Application/further learning. The learning never ends. What starts with a demonstration of a given skill ends with a demonstration of a related skill, which leads to further speculation, etc. Thus, skills acquisition can have a deliberate and meaningful place in learning.

However teachers decide to teach skills to students, it's important that they aim to achieve the following:

1. **Minimize phony lessons.** That is, teachers need to be sure that the worksheets, homework, and textbook pages they use and assign are carefully considered, rather than amounting to busy work having no significant purpose. It's wrongheaded to think that reams of exercises will best help students acquire skills. (Most students complete reams of exercises by copying a friend's work or by mechanically putting answers down on paper simply to complete the task so they can show their work is done.)

2. **Celebrate and study real language.** As often as you can, study skills in relation to the reading and writing students are actually doing rather than resorting to manufactured exercises.

3. **Seize the teaching opportunity.** Don't be afraid to drop the lesson at hand when an opportunity for teaching something of interest presents itself in your classroom. For instance, when an impromptu discussion on the overuse of the word *like* came up in our class, one student commented, "I like, like like." We immediately dissected the use: Which "like" is a verb? Which is the noun? And which is used, like, as an interjection?

Alternative Activity: Whatever . . . From A to Z

Grade: 7–8; also useful for 9–12
Time: One class period
Outcome: In writing, students brainstorm, sort, and organize their thoughts and knowledge about any topic.

This chapter's alternative activity is much like the one in Chapter 1; it's a very simple way to engage students in thinking, writing, and sharing. Have students compose an A to Z list, individually or in groups, on any topic they or you choose. Some examples: Greek Mythology From A to Z; The Harlem Renaissance From A to Z; *The Odyssey* From A to Z. The possibilities are endless, but these lists are especially good for prewriting or review.

Here are two lists a group of students recently composed. We used the first list for a whole-class vocabulary lesson; we used the second, more playful list as (1) a way for students to vent their frustration about a former social studies teacher's archaic methods and (2) for studying basic language mechanics: Which is an interrogative sentence? Which phrase is an example of hyperbole? Which phrase is an adverb–adjective combination? etc.

THREE-LETTER WORDS FROM A TO Z

Apt	Nil
Bop	Opt
Cur	Pip
Dud	Quo
Ewe	Rue
Fop	Sty
Gig	Tut
Hex	Ugh
Irk	Vim
Jut	Wan
Ken	Xox
Lax	Yen
Mow	Zen

THE HORROR OF FILMSTRIPS, A–Z

Annoying	Nervous breakdown
Boring	Obviously pathetic
Constant	Pollute your brain
Depressing	Questions that can't be
Every student's nightmare	answered
Flee the room!	Reality doesn't exist
Gather useless information	Slow death
Help! I'm afraid of the dark!	Teacher's break
Irritating	Until tomorrow . . .

Just remember
Keep a straight face
Like hell I'm going to enjoy it
Man's greatest enemy

Voodoo power
What's the point?
X-scape
Yell for mercy
Zombie's pleasure

4

The Vocabulary Conundrum

"I coagulated, and then I went home."
—Danielle Jenkins

$Consider$ this scenario: It's Monday morning and you've arrived a few minutes early to class to put the week's list of vocabulary words on the board. As you carefully transfer the list of words, you mentally calculate the week's agenda for your students:

Monday	Copy and preview a new set of words
Tuesday	Look up and study definitions
Wednesday	Compose sentences with the new words
Thursday	Review sentences and correct usage
Friday	Take a quiz on new vocabulary

Language teachers have long used this model to teach vocabulary: to increase word familiarity and expand word knowledge. It worked more or less for us as students, and we in turn carry on a similar routine approach. We design activities that require student participation; we require that they internalize the words—use them. Our intentions are noble, our efforts and labor intensive. We collect our words from the literature our students read or from lists supplied by the school district or from vocabulary books guaranteed to contain the words likely to appear on most standardized tests. Rather than reinvent the wheel, we use suggested vocabulary lists designated for appropriate levels. All this in combination makes logical sense. What results do we expect? What do we get?

Our students indicate anything from a slight distaste for learning words to a full-blown abhorrence. While this is unfortunate, like many things in life, we believe that if the medicine is to work, it may have to be distasteful. We've come to expect that it's natural for students to avoid or dislike word study—for them to find the process of learning new words tedious. And they often don't disappoint us.

Yet, there are successful alternative approaches to teaching vocabulary that go beyond using traditional vocabulary workbooks or textbooks that list words (before or at the end of chapters) for students to study.

How and Why We Teach Vocabulary the Way We Do

English teachers know that an extensive working vocabulary correlates with student success in school. The ability to retain and use words affects communication and comprehension in all disciplines; it's the common denominator—a thread that links all language skills. Facility with words gives us the ability to speak, listen, write, read, and think. As George Orwell surmised in his essay "Politics and the English Language," if we clarify our language, we can clarify our thinking. So it's understandable why we emphasize vocabulary in any curriculum. And yet an irony exists in how we present words to students. We've routinely and unintentionally emphasized the following tenets or behavior:

- A preoccupation with the number of words a student should acquire
- A reliance on memorized dictionary definitions
- A regular format of multiple-choice vocabulary tests
- A steady use of word drills and workbook exercises
- An assumption that prepackaged vocabulary lists are equally valuable to all students at a given grade level
- A notion that word recognition will lead to word usage

Good Intentions Versus Actual Results

Many teachers rely on vocabulary workbooks to provide or supplement word lists beyond what students encounter by reading literature or other required texts. With good intentions, teachers aim to expose students to new words and give them contextual practice with these words. Yet students see another objective: get through the exercises and fill in the blanks as quickly as possible. We typically don't give much attention to increasing the number of encounters students have with a word or don't consider the effect of a personal rewriting of a word's definition. Generally, dictionary definitions look like this:

co·ag·u·late (ko-àg¹ye-lât´) verb
co·ag·u·lat·ed, co·ag·u·lat·ing, co·ag·u·lates verb,
transitive

1. make or become semisolid: to thicken, or cause liquid to thicken, into a soft semisolid mass
2. group together in larger mass: to group together as a mass, or cause the particles in a colloid to group together

What do many students do with this definition? They study it—maybe memorize all the entries—and can recall the words in the definition for a quiz, provided the quiz uses the *same* words as the dictionary definition. Occasionally, we ask students to use the word in an original sentence. Many students react in one of three ways:

1. They choose the *first* definition.
2. They choose the *first definition they understand* or can apply to their own experience.
3. They choose the *appropriate definition* but *misuse* the word.

It's not surprising to find a sentence like this written by a student: *I coagulated, and then I went home.*

A student may argue that the sentence uses the word correctly, offering this explanation: in the afternoon we gather as a group at the bus lane, and then we go home. Attempts to explain a more appropriate use of a word can result in frustration, confusion or silent resignation by students more concerned about getting it right than "getting it." How can we increase the chances of a student using the word correctly in original writing? It will take a change in approach and expectations.

Promoting Word Consciousness

When students become familiar with words in more practical encounters, they learn to distinguish features of words that help them to use the words. This familiarity helps them to discriminate—to notice what, at first, they may have overlooked or weren't ready to see. Encounters with new words in context must be increased to gain this familiarity. Experimenting with the words, literally manipulating them and seeing them used in specific texts, will give students the experience they need. It's critical that the words exist beyond a list on the board or a page in a notebook.

What can teachers do to promote word consciousness and immerse students in language? First, dramatically supplement the traditional methods we use to teach vocabulary. These practical alternatives can change the prevailing attitude towards word acquisition and create situations in which students develop a need to know. It's possible to give students more control over learning new words. We should design instruction concerned with developing a heightened word consciousness, cultivating curiosity about word meanings, encouraging effective and memorable usage, and allowing independent analysis.

Cultivating Curiosity: Vocabulary Illustrations

One activity that achieves these objectives is creating a vocabulary illustration. These word illustrations made by students and displayed in the classroom can have lasting positive results. Vocabulary illustrations take time to produce—a necessary factor that gives students time to manipulate and practice with words on their own. The final product can easily undergo revision. The directions for producing a vocabulary illustration are simple and adaptable. Here are suggested directions for creating one.

Vocabulary Illustrations
    Grade: 7–12
    Time: One class session; ongoing
    Outcome: Promoting vocabulary growth and retention

On unlined paper create an attractive, interesting vocabulary illustration using these four steps:

    1. Find a picture or use an original drawing that illustrates the word and helps to define it as it is used.
    2. Write and include a clear definition of the word.
    3. Highlight the word at least three times, using contrasting colors, different font types/sizes or eye-catching hand lettering.
    4. Use the word in an original sentence that relates to the picture and helps to define the word.

Note: By using this class collaborative effort, a list of twenty or more words can be divided among the class so that each student is responsible for one or two words to incorporate in an illustration. It defeats the purpose of the assignment to assign each student all the words or too many words.

These hints will help you guide students in this activity:

- A vocabulary illustration is *not* an exact picture of a word or an exact visual representation. (This would limit the activity and change the focus to searching for pictures that literally *define* words, often a near impossibility.)
- The picture or illustration should be suggestive, related or connected in a way that helps define the word. (This makes the term memorable for students.)
- An illustration should exhibit creativity, imagination, use of color, and decorative lettering. (This ensures investment in each selected word.)

Many students find it easier to use, understand, and recall new vocabulary words after they've created their own vocabulary illustration. They've spent time with words, manipulating and learning them. Students actually enjoy acquiring new words and internalize meanings and appropriate usage in the process. With a few old magazines, glue, paper, and colored markers, students can begin to play around with words in a variety of ways. A sample vocabulary illustration is shown in Figure 4–1.

When teachers surround students with word illustrations that visually appeal to them, word consciousness, comprehension, and retention increase. As students read and compare illustrations, they begin to see nuances in definitions and usage. They make necessary connections between words and the images they evoke. Rather than writing unfamiliar words in nonsensical sentences, students make decisions on how words are best used for effect. The visual illustrations reinforce meaning in ways that workbook exercises can't. Students approach new words in ways that work for them.

Finding Definitions in Pictures

Brett, a high school junior, often sat in homeroom slumped over the desk with his head resting on his arms. From his reclining vantage point he stared blankly at vocabulary illustrations taped to the walls.

Brett's revelation came one Monday morning after he had taken the SATs. He arrived in class looking more alert than usual and announced, "You're not going to believe this. You know those vocabulary posters hanging up around here? Well, there must have been at least ten of those words on the SAT, and I knew them!"

QUINTESSENCE

QUINTESSENCE — NOUN. — The pure, highly concentrated essence of something

A rose is the QUINTESSENCE of beauty.

QUINTESSENCE

FIGURE 4–1. Vocabulary illustration 1

Anecdotal evidence being what it is, we're not suggesting that by just having word illustrations on the walls in a classroom that all students will internalize and learn new vocabulary without effort, but this story confirms several important points:

- Vocabulary acquisition doesn't have to be painful.
- Language is best learned and retained by long-term, repeated exposure to it.
- Learning new vocabulary can be a natural function of seeing and hearing words.
- There's a need for flexibility in how we present new vocabulary to students.

Brett's story supports the positive effect alternative approaches to vocabulary acquisition can have on students. Added to traditional methods of word study, vocabulary illustrations, even unintentionally, result in learning.

Extending the Strategy: Vocabulary Illustration Journals

Another adaptation of this activity that gives students control over acquiring new words is producing a vocabulary journal. This type of journal encourages critical thinking and independent study. Here are several possibilities for creating illustration journals.

Grade: 7–12
Time: Two to three class sessions; ongoing
Outcome: Students create vocabulary journals

Design an imaginative journal project that will give students an opportunity to gain control over their vocabulary study in an independent way. In these journals, students should compile a list of appropriate words (which can be selected from specific texts or lists), select appropriate ones, and organize this grouping of words so that each word contributes to a single focus.

- Group students giving them the task of producing a journal of vocabulary illustrations using new vocabulary centered around a single idea, topic, or theme—for example, friendship, injustice, isolation.
- Select a character from literature and using vocabulary illustrations compile a character profile—for example, create illustrations for a journal to characterize Holden Caulfield, Huck Finn, or Boo Radley.

- Create a journal of vocabulary illustrations that focuses on a career, an occupation, or specific field of interest, such as computer science, horticulture, or ballet.

The journal pages can be displayed on a poster or bound in a folder. These personalized journals provide students and parents with excellent evidence of vocabulary development, acquisition, and use. The strength of the journal activity is that students have ownership of vocabulary. They see words unified by a concept they have identified; they see a practical application for these words.

The Way Words Work

A collaborative activity that engages students, immerses them in language and leads to a shared piece of writing is the Word Factory. The activity is divided into three phases; it allows students to play with words and learn them in the process. The activity requires that students use and rearrange the letters from "base words" to produce new ones. For example, from the letters in the word *coagulate* students might create the following new words: teal, goat, locate, local, etc.

In the first phase of this activity, students acquire a group of words (base words) to use later in producing new words. They do this as groups competing against each other in the class in a "Word Auction." From selected lists of words (you can use vocabulary lists or words from literature, etc.), groups of students bid on and acquire base words. It is best to use several short lists of words—they can be written on the board so that all the groups can view them before the auction. They can make choices about which words they would like to acquire. They need to know that they will be using the letters from each word to form new words a little later on, so they should be encouraged to bid on and obtain the "best" words. They quickly figure out that base words that are long and have a variety of letters are the most useful. Be sure the lists contain a variety of types of words. Each group member can be involved in the auction as a bidder, recorder, or statistician.

The auction requires that students actively take part in acquiring the words they will use in the production phase. The roles can be rotated during each round of bidding. Give each group a limited number of points (100 works well) and run the auction similarly to the way an auctioneer would. Announce each word up for bid, one at a time, designating the bidding as round 1, round

2, and so on. Evenly distribute them—so that all the "good" words don't appear in one round of the auction:

Phase 1: Word Auction Lists

I	II	III
rub	incessant	desolate
extend	motionless	marred
sustain	scent	undisturbed
quietly	discarded	clusters
loosened	brisk	precious
flutter	desire	irritable

The groups use their points to acquire their words—keeping track of the points they've expended and perhaps saving points to bid on an especially useful word in a later round. While this auction is not central to the purpose of the activity, it's important for students to have some freedom to choose their words and have some fun in the process. It represents a distinctive difference in how vocabulary words have been typically introduced to them. It proves to be worth the time and effort.

After the groups have acquired their base words in the auction—using their points—phase 2 begins with each group deciding how to best handle the task of producing new words with the letters from each word they have obtained. Like in a real factory, the objective is to produce products. In this second phase of the activity, each group attempts to produce the most new words possible from the letters they have, using only the letters in each word. (It defeats the activity if they pool all the letters from all the words.) Agreeing to a limited amount of time, allow the groups to work and make new words.

Phase 2: Word Factory

Objectives

1. Use the words in the Word Auction (base words) as your raw material to create new words.
2. Produce original words using the letters in the base words.
3. Produce a collaborative piece of writing using as many of the newly created words as possible.
4. Score points for
   - Acquiring as many words as possible in the auction
   - Using all your bank of points in the auction
   - Producing the most words from the letters in each base word

- Creating the longest word
- Using "newly formed" words in your final writing
5. Deduct points for
   - Not using all auction points
   - Illegal, misspelled, or nonwords

Groups

1. Agree upon a method for creating new words cooperatively.
2. Create new words from base words (you can double/triple letters in each word).
3. Total all your points for new words created (one point /letter in each word).
4. Decide upon and write a final original piece of writing.

Auction points

Each group begins the auction with 100 points to use for bidding on the list(s) of words. Each group should try to devise a plan to use all their points or most of them during the auction to acquire base words. Deduct unused points from the group's score.

Example: If group 3 bids on words and uses 87 points of their 100—they begin the manufacturing process with a –13.

Point chart

Each letter used in each newly formed word counts for one point. Of course, the group's goal is to create as many words in the time limit, especially long ones, to score the most points.

Example: Base word (acquired in the auction) FACTORY

TRACTOR	=	7 pts
TAFFY	=	5 pts
FACT	=	4 pts
FACE	=	–4 pts (illegal—no "e" in base word)
CAT	=	3 pts
TO	=	2 pts

After groups have produced new words from the letters that formed their base words and totaled their points, you should reward the top group and others in some way—extra credit points, a classwork grade, or some other appropriate action to give credit for work well done. Trading newly created word lists among groups and having one group check the validity of another group's total is an easy way to ensure accuracy.

The third phase requires that students select words from those they created and use them in an original piece of writing. This writing is the ultimate objective of this activity.

Phase 3: Final Products

Choose and use as many appropriate words that you've purchased and created to write an original group product. This will be a collaborative piece of writing, so everyone in the group should have input in creating the piece and revising it. Share your final product with the entire class.

POSSIBLE OPTIONS

1. News article
2. Short story
3. Poem
4. Front page of a newspaper
5. Fairy tale
6. Speech
7. Manual
8. Recipe
9. Letter
10. Advertisement
11. Commercial
12. Play
13. Directions
14. Exam
15. Creative essay
16. Children's story
17. Song
18. News script
19. Biography
20. Interview

Phase 3 is evaluated, to some degree, on the number of words woven into an original piece of writing but more on the quality of the final piece. Sharing, distributing, or displaying these products in a creative class presentation is an excellent culminating activity. Groups and individual should be rewarded for collaboratively producing a good piece of writing. There are many ways to reward students for the work they did in the groups; this encourages cooperative work on future assignments for which you may want a group effort.

Alternative Activity: Word Find

Grade: 7–12
Time: Part of one class session; ongoing
Outcome: Promoting independent deep structure revision

The Word Find activity offers students options for generating or revising their writing. The strategy can be adapted for use throughout the writing process when students want to generate more words to choose from as they write. Student writers develop lists of words to draw upon before they write, as they write, or after they've written a piece. It's effective and economical.

Tip for success: Students need not use every word they generate; this will discourage them from using this strategy. Students will generate or find many more words than they will use.

Word Find Writing Options

Directions. Use several texts as sources to collect words for each of these options. Subject textbooks, popular magazines, and newspapers will work fine. It is preferable to use texts unrelated to your topic or idea. (You may find it useful, though, to adapt this technique by using texts that *do* pertain to the topic you are writing about. Try both.) Use a highlighter to make your selections or a pen and paper to copy your choices. Choose a good number of words by simply listing them; the strategy works best when you select words that might "possibly" be used in a piece of writing. Choose from the following options.

Option 1. Find a piece or several pieces of writing (your sources) from which you can select words to create a list. Look for words you like or that appeal to you. This should not be a search for difficult or unknown vocabulary terms. Randomly group or list these selected words to make it easy for you to read them later.

After your search, review your list(s). Let a *topic or central idea emerge* based on an impression you get from several words or groups of words. Write a piece in which you use several words from your list. Use the words from these lists to supplement your writing rather than trying to use *all* the words. Write it in a readable form ready for sharing. Title it.

Option 2. Think of a *roughly formed topic or idea* that you want to write about. If you are interested in writing about a person or place indicate that on a piece of paper as a focus point. Once you've established this, go *word shopping.*

Select words that might work for your piece. Choose words related to your topic. Create a bank of possible words to use in your original piece. Write about your selected topic using several selected words from your list. Title it.

Option 3. Choose a piece of *writing that you have written* in draft form. Read the draft to refresh your memory of the word choices you made. Select a piece of writing other than your own, and go word shopping. Collect words that you might possibly add or substitute for words in the original draft. Your intent is to enhance a piece already written. Shop quickly with the intention of finding words that will work in your piece. Use some of these words to revise your draft.

Word-find self-assessment. Respond in writing (about a paragraph long) how the word find option you selected specifically worked for you. Include this with your piece.

Tip for success. If you use this activity as a tool to strengthen or revise writing, you might consider asking students to practice all three options. Later, they can choose the technique that works best for them and their writing style.

The effort to improve students' vocabulary is one that we should attend to in *every* writing and language activity. We must find palatable ways to focus on language and words so that students will develop a facility with learning words. It's important to try a variety of alternative methods and not let the success or failure of teaching vocabulary rest upon one approach. Often the subtle methods by which we incorporate words in our classroom activities have the most profound effects. When students accept the importance of an increased personal vocabulary and feel a real need for learning words, the effort becomes most effective. We should be alert to any methods or activities that promote these conditions. The power we give students who are able to recognize, retain, and use words effectively has far-reaching returns. Fundamental success in school depends on it.

5
Designing Workshop Classrooms

"Free from the bonds of teachers, so that you can teach yourself."
—*Dave Harris*

A workshop classroom is one where the teacher plans enough time, on a regular basis, for students to engage in reading and writing activities, both individually and cooperatively, often across the disciplines. It incorporates curriculum requirements into a setting where students have time to process and show whatever tasks, skills, or concepts drive that curriculum. They have time in class to read and write in the presence of a teacher who acts more as coach than lecturer, responding to student needs as they arise and spending less time on full-period lectures. Instead, on "workshop" days, the teacher gives a brief introduction or mini-lesson (five to nine minutes) and sets the students to work. Students must take on more responsibility for the quality and direction of their own learning.

Teachers know the value of classroom workshops and incorporate them regularly into their plans in a variety of efficient and effective ways. Some desire a break from the teacher-centered lessons that have become tiresome or have yielded too little student response or work but may be fearful of losing control of the students or the curriculum or both. Though they might agree with a classroom-as-workshop approach, they need specific structures and suggestions—and some reassurance—to get them started.

At least in part, English teachers associate the writing workshop (or writers' workshop) and the reading workshop (readers' workshop) with Atwell's *In the Middle* (1997). Many teachers value the book as the guiding principle for reading and writing workshops in their classes.

Think of workshop classrooms in an open way; a narrow or absolute determination about what "workshop" is can get in the way of its use. A successful workshop can take on many different approaches and configurations; teachers and students are not limited to any one way. Workshops can succeed in every educational grouping or setting.

As well, teachers and students will effect changes in the structures of workshop classrooms as needs of all kinds—internally found or externally imposed—arise. A middle school classroom is a good example. Workshops ten years ago centered almost exclusively on individual reading and writing choices. Now, English and social studies teachers are sometimes assigned the same students and a common schedule. In adjoining classrooms where a folding wall creates one large space, workshop often means interdisciplinary projects.

We've organized the chapter both topically and chronologically so that all teachers can find something valuable. Use this chapter to help design classroom workshops to start a school year or to infuse a classroom with workshops during the school year.

Starting the School Year

In our classrooms, reading/writing workshops as a type of class structure begin about five weeks into the school year. Likewise, we suggest that teachers begin their school year by laying the foundation for workshops without making a big deal—or any mention at all—of the concept of workshop or their plans for enacting it.

Instead, for the first five weeks of school, we lay the foundation for workshop classes by creating an environment where the structure of each class is clear and expectations are definite, but where student choice (using a reader response journal rather than completing study questions, for example) is valued.

The first month of school is a time for introducing and practicing the skills students will need in order to succeed at workshop—including free writing, silent reading, finding and using materials, and group work—a little at a time. Most times, it's not a good idea to celebrate the notion of freedom too early in the school year. Students need to learn that they have to do what the teacher says.

It's a good time to read a novel, combining at-home reading assignments with silent reading and reading aloud in class, using reader response techniques and reading check quizzes. Students will know that English class means work. Then, once good work habits are established and healthy interpersonal relationships begin to form, the teacher can effectively introduce workshops. Students still have to do what the teacher tells them to do—but the teacher allows an increasingly larger arena of possibilities as students show that they're ready.

Note the six components of our English class, which help prepare students for workshop classes to come:

1. *Free Writing.* This is the first thing students do on the first day of school. Ken Macrorie's definition of free writing in *Writing to Be Read* (1984) works well for students of all ages.

Write freely for twelve minutes as fast as you can, still being legible, never stopping to ponder a thought or to consider spelling, punctuation, or grammar. Put down whatever comes to mind. If you find you can't get started, look in front of you or out the window and begin describing whatever you see. Let yourself wander to different subjects, feelings, or ideas, but keep writing. Aim to fill at least one full page. Remember, you are hitting practice shots, not writing to impress anyone—nothing phony or fake or designed to make you look good.

Students receive a sheet of yellow paper and begin writing. (Yellow paper—as opposed to white—indicates that the piece is a draft; and having students free write on individual sheets rather than in a journal facilitates easy collection.) We sometimes tell students that if they complete the task as assigned, they will have received their first "A" of the year; we collect the papers and read them, making not a single mark on any paper. When their writing folders (for drafts and works in progress) are labeled and ready, we put this piece and all other such pieces into the folders for future use and reference.

Done on the first day of school, this activity immediately establishes writing as important and freedom of expression as the tone of the class. It allows students some introspective and creative time on a day when most teachers spew rules at them ad nauseum. It gives the teacher an immediate writing sample and a first insight into each student. Thereafter, students free write as an activity once a week or so for twelve minutes.

Free writing refers to the students' approach to writing, not necessarily to freedom of topic. Use the concept of directed free writing for times when students should freely and fully respond to a given topic. Note these further suggestions:

- Avoid giving students prompts and suggestions when they free write, especially at the start of the school year or if the concept is new to them.
- Free writing does not always mean that students pick their own topics; it also applies to times when students respond freely to a given topic. For example, the teacher might ask students to write freely

when evaluating their own progress in the workshop or when writing an autobiographical sketch. The topic is given, but the approach is free.

- Once a workshop mode is in place, free writing will occur intermittently, a student at a time, not only as an assigned activity.

2. Notebook Entries. It's important that students keep a notebook, properly labeled with dates and titles, for mini-lessons on workshop days or for lengthier notes that a full-period lesson might require. These notes should take on a variety of forms: outlines, lists, short paragraphs, semantic maps, etc.

3. Reading Aloud. One of the best things a teacher can do is read aloud to students—either a portion of the book they're studying together, or perhaps a shorter piece for discussion and response. Students love to hear their teacher present literature aloud. Furthermore, the teacher models the phrasing, dynamics, and even questioning techniques that students will infuse into their own reading, maybe without consciously knowing it. When the teacher pauses (we suggest sparingly) for questioning, asking students to recap or predict, or note character growth, students infuse their own reading with similar questions.

4. USSR. Have students read silently, without interruption, for twenty or thirty minutes. This will let them know that sometimes, quiet reading will be in order—that the actual reading, and not questioning or discussion—*is* the work. Let students choose any available materials you have in class; don't limit them to the assigned novel only. (Here, too, teachers can choose to offer an "A" to any student who successfully completes the silent reading task.) By requiring students to read without interruption but allowing them to choose what they read, teachers present the "freedom within structure" framework that will make future workshops successful.

Tip for success. Once a workshop scheme is in place, teachers need to help students get used to reading and writing quietly even when all is not quiet around them.

5. Reading Assignments, Checks, and Reader Response. In addition to having students start a reader response journal (see Chapter 1), it's a good idea to give two or three definite reading assignments and announced quizzes on those assignments. By doing so, teachers can balance the grades students may have earned by engaging in the process of reading or writing with grades that measure their reading comprehension or tell whether they've completed the required reading. In this way, the teacher uses both traditional methods and reader response techniques in preparing students for workshop classes.

6. A *Simple Activity.* It's a good idea to have students complete a simple activity (two or three class periods) shortly after the school year starts. If students are seated in groups of four while they complete individual activities, they work both individually and cooperatively as they ask each other for opinions and advice. The teacher can watch students work, move from group to group, and comment sparingly as he sets the tone for students to produce. An example of such an activity follows.

Writing and Illustrating Change Poems

> **Grade:** 7–12, especially appropriate for interdisciplinary topics
> **Time:** Approximately two class periods
> **Outcome:** Students think in terms of opposites, growth, and change. They write and illustrate original poems depicting change suitable for display.

This activity allows students to show their thought processes in simple, accessible poetry. We adapted the activity from Joseph I. Tsujimoto's *Teaching Poetry Writing to Adolescents* (1988) by having students illustrate and graphically present their poems on 6″ × 18″ white drawing paper.

Directions: Write a poem describing a single change or multiple changes using one-word lines and stanzas.

1. Brainstorm topics. Think of words, changes, and movements through time: for example, infant to teenager. Think of nouns, both abstract and concrete. Think in terms of opposites: life/death; beginning/end.
2. Play with words.
3. Draft and write.
4. Design a display copy of your final poem. Consider lettering, simple illustration, and overall artistic effect. (See Figure 5–1.)

Creating a Reading/Writing Workshop

Designing a workshop classroom is both creative and imitative. Readers of this book will combine its models and suggestions with others, making modifications and adding their own styles. There's no exact formula for creating a reading/writing workshop—the structure depends upon what curriculum and

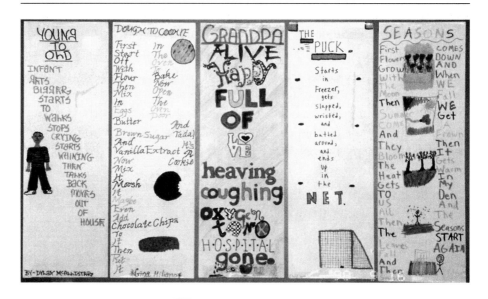

FIGURE 5–1. Illustrated Changed Poems

students the teacher is dealing with. Teachers should consider the following questions of workshop management as they gather materials and put their programs together:

1. How much time will you devote to each segment of the workshop?
2. Where will books (and other reading materials), folders, and materials be?
3. How and when will students get their materials?
4. How will you begin each workshop session?
5. What are the rules going to be during the reading and writing time itself?
6. How often will you integrate required reading into workshops?
7. Where, when, how will conferences (teacher–student and student–student) take place?
8. How will students share their writings?
9. How will you publish students' writing and provide students with an audience?
10. What problems can you predict?

In designing our first month's classes, we've already shown students a good deal of what the workshop is. When we're ready to introduce workshops, it's time to tell them about the reading/writing workshop. We don't begin with past students' assessments or testimonials. Instead, we put these simple notes on the board and discuss them:

READING/WRITING WORKSHOP

1. What is a reading/writing workshop? It's a method of organizing class and classwork that encourages freedom, choice, and responsibility.
2. How is a workshop class organized?
   - Introduction/minilesson: five to eight minutes
   - Workshop time: thirty minutes
   - Wrap-up/Cleanup: two to five minutes
3. How often will we have a workshop? An average of three times a week

In discussing these notes with students, we tell them that on workshop days, they will enter the room and see *Today: Reading/Writing Workshop* on the easel or chalkboard. On these days especially, they must tune in immediately for the mini-lesson, which will take fewer than ten minutes, after which they can work for a half hour without any teacher lecturing and minimal teacher interruption. The mini-lesson is not a time for student questions that would be better asked and addressed during the workshop half hour itself.

Mini-lessons in our classroom include a wide variety of topics, including (but not limited to) the following:

- A list or explanation of things students might consider doing in the workshop that day: book talks, materials choices, etc.
- A sharing of what students are accomplishing during workshop time
- Notes and discussion of any issue, topic, or skill germane to students' work in workshop
- Notes and discussion of topics related to "nonworkshop" days
- Reading aloud and brief discussion (perhaps using one or two of the "varied approaches" found in Chapter 1) of a poem of interest
- Reading aloud of a book excerpt, article, brief short story, etc.

Tip for success. We established the week of plans included as a model in Chapter 3 (see Figure 3–1) in October, right after implementing reading/writing workshops in class. It illustrates how mini-lessons can function: on Monday, the teacher presented workshop choices and logistics; on Wednesday, the teacher finished a discussion of irony after Tuesday's whole-class lesson on Shirley Jackson's "Charles"; and on Thursday, the teacher gave a mini-lesson about free writing and the logistics of using writing folders (this type of mini-lesson is most common early in the school year, but necessary throughout).

Note again: Some teachers conduct reading and writing workshops separately and on given days each week. For example, writing workshops on Monday and Friday, reading workshops on Tuesday and Thursday, whole-class lessons on Wednesday. We suggest that rather than locking into days that might not fit into your school calendar, assembly schedule, and personal schedule, teachers should plan workshops as they fit—but with a steadfast commitment to more than once a week. If during one week students get only two workshops, plan for three the next week. A predictable schedule is good, but flexibility is key.

After we've discussed these notes, we distribute and discuss Expectations for Reading/Writing Workshop, a handout for students and their parents that incorporates some of Nancie Atwell's suggested aims for writing workshop (1987) with our own. The handout is divided into three parts:

- Your roles and responsibilities as a student
- My roles and responsibilities as your teacher
- Required assignments for all students

We print these expectations on neon-colored sheets for easy finding; we give parents copies on open school night, and students keep copies in their writing folder. Use whatever parts fit your needs:

EXPECTATIONS FOR READING/WRITING WORKSHOP
YOUR ROLES AND RESPONSIBILITIES AS A STUDENT:

1. Take care of and use your writing folder.
2. Read and write every day.
3. Try all different kinds of reading and writing.
4. Write in your Reader Response Journal regularly—at least one thoughtful entry per week. Write in response to the works we read in class and in response to your own reading choices.
5. Plan your reading and writing; work on them in class and at home.
6. In addition to doing a careful job on assigned topics, find topics that you care about, and write about those things—in poetry or in prose.
7. Revise, edit, and finish pieces of writing. Neatly write or process final manuscripts. Use proper margins.
8. Number and date your drafts of each piece.
9. Work hard at self-editing your drafts—use a colored pencil or marker.
10. Take care of all resources and materials that I've provided.
11. Make decisions about what's working and what needs more attention in your reading and writing. Listen to and question other writers' pieces, giving thoughtful, helpful response.
12. Do not do anything to disturb or distract the teacher or other writers.

And discover the reader and writer inside you—discover what reading and writing can do for you.

MY ROLES AND RESPONSIBILITIES AS YOUR TEACHER:

1. Keep track of your reading and writing and what you need as a reader and writer.
2. Grade your writing at least four times this year, based on growth, effort, and the quality of your final pieces.
3. Read and write every day.
4. Prepare and present mini-lessons based on what I see you need to know.
5. Help you find books and topics you care about.

6. Provide a predictable class structure in which you'll feel free to be able to grow as a reader and writer.

7. Organize the classroom to meet your needs as a reader and writer.

8. Give you opportunities to enter contests, display your writing, and publish your writing.

9. Teach you specific reading and writing skills.

10. Provide you with reading and writing materials.

11. Listen to you and respond to your writing by asking thoughtful, helpful questions.

12. Make sure no one disturbs you or distracts you when you're reading, writing, or conferring.

REQUIRED ASSIGNMENTS FOR ALL STUDENTS:

- Literary essays/related writing: *Across Five Aprils* by Irene Hunt— Due: _____
- Book review—Due: _____
- Autobiographical piece—Due: _____
- At least one finished, polished piece of your choice—Due: ____

Note these points of interest about our "Expectations for Reading/Writing Workshop":

1. We are creating an environment where students write for more than grades. We do not grade each piece of writing. Rather, we grade writing and assess writing skills and progress sparingly—on selected assignments only, and on a quarterly basis. Students need to take responsibility for evaluating the quality of their own writing.

2. Students keep two folders during the course of the year, located in two accessible file drawers in the classroom: the first is the writing folder already mentioned, which is used for keeping assignment sheets, writing inventories, outlines and lists, free writing, works in progress, and so on. The second is a portfolio where we keep all graded or finished assignments, including short answer quizzes, pieces of writing, and storable projects.

3. We use this second portfolio folder regularly during the school year for both formal and informal assessments (see "An Activity for Midyear Assessment" later in this chapter) and extensively for the final portfolio discussed in Chapter 10.

4. Because is it nearly impossible for an English teacher to grade everything a student writes—and because doing so does not

encourage students to evaluate their own writing as they progressively review their portfolios—it's a mistake to put grades on all pieces of writing.

5. The "Required Assignments for All Students" section includes requirements for the second half of October, November, and December. Designed for heterogeneously grouped eighth-grade classes, these requirements are sparse by design, neither easy nor overwhelming. However, they are basic requirements, not ultimate requirements; many students accomplish more by completing several polished pieces or several book reviews (written on 5″ × 8″ index cards) for our classroom file.

6. Not all student writing is represented in the "Required assignments for all students" section. The reader response journal and free writing, for example, are important components of a beginning workshop experience.

Teachers of upper-level classes in grades 11 and 12 (even honors classes) might resist planning too many assignments for workshop time—though they may well need to assign more than a teacher of eighth-grade classes assigns.

To accompany such an "Expectations for Reading/Writing Workshop" sheet, teachers might like to compose a letter to parents as a way of giving a more personal introduction or explanation of how the class will proceed for the year. Here's an excerpt from the letter we give to parents several weeks into the school year:

> Dear Parents,
>
> In English class, we will use a Reading/Writing Workshop approach throughout the year. Please read the neon handout provided. Until mid-January or February, we will be studying short works of literature together, but we will not be studying books together as a class. My experience in teaching thirteen- and fourteen-year-olds tells me that if I handed out required book after required book, "school" books like the one we're just finishing (*Across Five Aprils*), I would stunt their reading growth rather than promote it. Your sons and daughters are at the age where the most important thing they can do to serve themselves as students and as learners and as interesting people is read, read, read—all kinds of things. So, for the next three months, they will choose their own books.
>
> Homework in English this year will consist primarily of reading, writing, and occasionally interviewing or studying. While the focus of our year will not be the rote learning of spelling, vocabulary, and grammar, we will integrate these with our reading and writing, and students will receive

periodic quizzes in these areas. They will need to study in order to do well. You should see regular—almost daily—reading and writing occurring at home, just as I expect to see regular reading and writing occurring here at school.

The best way for you as parents to know what your son or daughter's specific homework assignments are is to request that s/he keep a running assignment book. Ask to see it however often you need to.

There are three main places to look if you want to see the specific work that your child is doing: the notebook/reader response journal, the writing folder (used for works in progress), and the portfolio (graded assignments, quizzes, and finished products are kept here for periodic review in class and for use in our final portfolio project in the spring). Writing folders and portfolios are stored here in class, but they are available for your son or daughter to show you—and use—at home.

I hope this letter and the accompanying handout are helpful to you. Good luck and best wishes as you carry out what I know is a difficult and daunting responsibility—parenting.

Some Hints to Make the Workshop Method Work

1. Operate with faith and determination: commit to three half-hour workshops a week. Integrate workshops with successful working practices without sacrificing the essence of what a workshop is.
2. Structure the learning environment, not (all) the learning activities; give students realms of choice that correspond with grade-level aims and requirements.
3. Maintain organization—ascribe a predictable structure to workshops even as you vary the activities.
4. Keep records, but don't go nuts. Make sure any rubrics or checklists you choose are clear and easy for you and students to use. Assess students' progress in skills holistically in the context of their work, but also require students to complete concrete skills assignments. One basic assignment every week or two will suffice. Grade these assignments—you'll appreciate having definite grades to complement the holistic assessments. Remember, all grading, testing, and assessment is subjective: any "objective" test or quiz you administer is "subject" to your choice.
5. Learn to negotiate—in your own mind—a fair way to accommodate differences in what students do. Not all students need to do the exact same writing, complete the exact same assignments, or have the same number of grades for each marking period.

6. You do not need to read or respond to everything every student writes. Encourage students to rely on each other for reading and response.

7. Move about the room and conduct quick, impromptu conferences. You're a sitting duck if you conduct individual conferences by having students report to you at your seat.

8. Control the tenor of workshop classes. Sometimes you'll need to insist on a quiet setting. If students have little reason to confer (or no drafts to confer about), or if they need to engage in reading, you'll want to minimize sharing. On the other hand, if workshops are continually quiet and students are reluctant to revise or edit their work together, you'll want to designate some days for conference or revision, insisting that students share their work.

9. Don't let students get away with a fake sharing and assessment. Taking hold of a classmate's writing for thirty seconds or so and saying, "That's good," and returning the piece without reading it, doesn't give it serious consideration.

10. Have students read their work aloud to one another. Have the author come up with a specific question or two she wants the listener to consider as she reads the piece aloud. Develop simple, specific questions students might like to use for this purpose (a perfect topic for a mini-lesson).

Finding and Nurturing Student Writers

During workshop time, the teacher conducts conferences and helps students, of course, but should not limit her activities to helping students who ask. The teacher's willingness and ability to present herself as a fellow reader and writer in their midst is a vital part of creating a workshop environment where students develop both independence and interdependence as readers and writers. It's not wrong for the teacher to say on a given workshop day, "I'm choosing my own agenda today, so I'm not available for questions or conferences," or "I have some writing of my own that I need to do during workshop today, so I want for you to rely on your classmates for help."

Now, the teacher can find and nurture student writers. It is perhaps the most rewarding thing about conducting workshops. The teacher has time to get a sense of students' reading and writing. While students are working, the teacher watches and responds. Or, while the students work, the teacher reads writing folders from a previous or forthcoming class to get a glimpse of their contents. This way, she can make a note to speak to a student about his reading or writing during their next workshop session. The teacher gets to experience students' reading and writing as it occurs; she offers responses while reading and writing is happening. (A class made up of teacher-centered lectures does not afford enough time for such responses to students' work, which have to take place during lunch, after school, or in between classes when students mob their teachers for a sliver of time and not much attention.)

Throughout the school year, it's enjoyable and rewarding to find student talent that the teacher will nurture. The teacher helps each student develop whatever abilities she can.

Such an opportunity came when a student named Joe scratched out a page of lines during workshop one day in response to a call for submissions to the Walt Whitman Birthplace Association's Twelfth Annual Student Poetry Contest (Theme: "Good Deeds, Indeed!"). Here's where the teacher was able to serve as editor—by posing careful questions in order to help the writer develop a piece and see it more fully:

- Have you achieved what you intended to achieve in the piece?
- Are you satisfied that your word choices create the right images, showing what you want them to show?
- Have you considered placement of words, phrases, lines, etc., or made such choices intuitively?
- Do you like the direction of the lines in your poem? Is anything missing?
- What does your poem need in order for you to consider it "whole"?

Questions like these can help the student process a piece. While the teacher poses them, she can be taking notes as the student responds—serving as both editor and transcriber while the student processes and verbalizes information.

Sometimes, too, a simple question can yield the perfect response. Joe's poem "The Osprey" is a good example. Simple questions posed by the teacher, like "Where's the captain?" and "What's he doing?" helped the writer supply detail and imagery. As well, the poem moved from first to third draft without a title, when the teacher asked, "Have you considered a title for your poem?"

When Joe answered, "No," she thought a while and asked a second question: "What's the name of the boat you're telling about?"

"The Osprey," Joe replied.

"Then there's your title."

Note the progression of the teacher's work with Joe as she helped him edit his work from first (Figure 5–2) to final draft.

Joe Rafanello

Bearing the Ropes + Rigging
On the water in the LI Sound
The money isn't too good
I work for free
The strong aroma of bluefish fills the air
Theres much to be done
fish left and right, "take this one

off the hook"   } Customers see
"$Measure this Bass"   only the ends
" not this fish"   of their rods
The way of the water in the back of my head
I sometimes get a chance to eat
rarely though
As the boat moves its strategic position
I watch the swirling water turn   VAGUE
A ~~faint~~ reflection resembles a
hardworking & person
The whole day I work
I Pound my energy into everything I do
The fish smell gets to you after awhile
Then again I must stop daydreaming
Theres work to be done
People yell
If the fising dosen't pick up customers won't
                                          come
we ~~need help~~ At the end of the day
~~Is there a fish got~~ I fillet fish
and And we pull into a sunset filled bay
        [wheelhouse
        fishfinder (looking)]

FIGURE 5–2. Osprey poem: draft 1 (Joe Rafanello)

77

Joe's first draft shows a few teacher edits based upon questioning the writer. His second draft, written during workshop time, shows a kind of "messing around with words." (See Figure 5–3.) This collaboration involved the teacher helping with word processing while the student edited the piece.

While no teacher should sit at the keyboard processing all students' work (it would be impossible anyway), it's an effective motivator for the teacher to show a reluctant student what his work could or might look like as a final manuscript. As well, it gives the teacher an opportunity to solicit further input from the student. That's what Figure 5–4 represents: his teacher showed Joe the draft, gave him a marker, and asked him to edit.

Here's the fourth and final draft of "The Osprey," a prize-winning poem:

THE OSPREY

Bearing the ropes and rigging
on the water in the LI Sound
I work for free.
The money isn't too good.
The captain's in the wheelhouse,
staring steady
through the fishfinder,
waiting for a passing school,
sipping coffee, quiet.

Strong aroma of bluefish,
fish left and right,
there's much to be done
while the fish come up.
Customers see
only the end of their rods:
Take this one off the hook.
Measure this bass, not this fish.
I sometimes get a chance to eat.
Rarely, though.

The Osprey moves
its strategic position,
a vague reflection resembling
the hard working person.
I watch the swirling water turn,
the way of the water
in the back of my head.

The whole day I work
I pound my energy into everything I do.
Fish smell gets to you after a while . . .

The captain's
in the wheelhouse,
staring steady
(1) through the fishfinder
waiting for a passing school,
quiet,
sipping coffee.

I work for free,
bearing the ropes and rigging
on the water in the LI Sound
The money isn't too good,
There's much to be done
Strong aroma of bluefish,
Fish left and right,
Customers

Strong aroma of bluefish,
Fish left and right,
I work for free,
bearing the ropes and rigging,
the way of

Bearing the ropes a/ rigging,
I work for free on the water
2   on the water
in the Long Island Sound.
The money isn't too good——
and there's much to be done,

(3)   Customers see only
the ends of their rods

FIGURE 5–3. Osprey poem: draft 2

Strong aroma of bluefish,

Fish left and right,

There's much to be done.
while the ~~close~~ fish come
Customers see

Only the end of their rods:

Take this one off the hook.

Measure this bass, not this fish.

I sometimes get a chance to eat.

Rarely, though.

Osprey
The ~~boat~~ moves

Its strategic position,

I watch the swirling water turn,

A vague reflection resembling

The hard-working person.

The way of the water

In the back of my head.

The whole day I work

I pound my energy into everything I do.

Fish smell gets to you after a while…

Then again,

I must stop daydreaming…

"Fish here!" people yell

At the end of the day

I filet fish
as
~~And~~ we pull into a sunset-filled bay.

FIGURE 5–4. Osprey poem: draft 3

Then again,
I must stop daydreaming . . .
"Fish here!" people yell

At the end of the day
I filet fish
as we pull into a sunset-filled bay.

Integrating Workshop Techniques with Standard Curriculum

At professional workshops and conferences, teachers often ask us to address this topic, and we think such integration is fairly simple to achieve. Given a five-day school week in which three are workshop classes, the teacher uses the remaining two classes to drive the curriculum.

Here's an example. If the class is reading and studying a novel, the teacher might hand out and introduce the book on Monday, reading aloud as far into Chapter 1 as time permits. On Tuesday, the teacher continues reading aloud, stopping as appropriate (not too seldom, not too often) for reactions, comments, and questions. Then the teacher can assign students to finish reading Chapter 1 by Friday, apprising them that Wednesday and Thursday will be workshop days. When students come to class on Wednesday and Thursday, many will use the time to continue reading the chapter. Some will have finished their reading the night before and will write a reader response entry into their journals. Others will report to class telling you that they're up to Chapter 3 or 4—that they couldn't put the book down. These students will either continue reading the book where they left off, happy for the chance, or they'll choose reading or writing beyond the novel assignments as their workshop pursuits. On Friday, the teacher can conduct a workshop class beginning with a mini-lesson in the form of a quiz, quick response to the book, discussion, or whatever she deems appropriate. If the teacher wants to forego the workshop on that day and continue reading Chapter 2 with students, she will offer three workshop sessions the following week.

Likewise, teachers can integrate given writing tasks into the workshop configuration. The teacher can introduce or present the assignment as a whole-class lesson or minilesson however she chooses; students can work on their writing both at home and during subsequent workshop classes. Students need to know that they will be most successful with the workshop if they work on their reading and writing both in school and at home. On workshop days, the teacher might offer a minilesson on topics germane to the completion of that assignment.

Following is a sample of a standard assignment that can be integrated into workshop time:

The Explanatory Composition (How to Accomplish Anything/Complete a Process)

Grade: 7–10
Time: Ongoing during workshop—approximately three weeks from introduction of assignment to student completion of final drafts
Outcomes: Students organize, write, revise, edit, and rewrite explanatory papers.

Directions. Write a well-developed multiparagraph piece that clearly explains how to complete a process. Consider the tone of your writing (serious, humorous, informative, etc.) so that it complements your topic and fits your audience.

Aims

- Select and limit a process.
- Explain the necessary steps chronologically.
- Use chronological transitions (procedural markers).
- Be precise and complete.

Think, outline if you want, write a first draft, revise and edit, write a second draft, revise and edit, prepare a proper final manuscript.

Choose (or adapt) one of the suggested topics below, or come up with one of your own:

HOW TO . . .

1. Get your way with Mom and/or Pop
2. Make a good impression on a date
3. Be a successful student
4. Play any one position in any one sport
5. Put together an outfit
6. Terrorize a sibling into submission
7. Plan a surprise party
8. Drive your teacher nuts
9. Fix a flat tire
10. Start a small business (child care, landscaping, and so on.)

11. Learn to ski
12. Write a composition

Mini-lessons to begin workshop days while students are working on their pieces might include the following:

- What it means to limit a topic
- Words that mark procedure or chronology: first, then, next, after that, finally, etc.
- Using commas after words, phrases, or clauses that function as procedural markers at the beginning of a sentence

Tips for success. When you use an assignment like the "How to" sample as part of your workshop plans, allow enough time for the students to process and perfect their work. If you require final copies soon after you give the assignment, you may be subverting the freedom—the choice element—of workshop. A few weeks is not automatically excessive, even though the assignment is a fairly simple one and not all students will need that much time. You want for the writings to exist in students' minds, at their desks, on their diskettes long enough to take root. As well, when you do come up with a due date, consider giving a due date window; for example, "Your *How to* pieces are due from Wednesday, January 20 to Friday, January 22. You may hand them in on any of those dates for full credit." And don't let students hand papers in any earlier.

An Activity for Midyear Assessment

Workshop classes lend themselves to students assessing themselves and each other, both informally and formally. Following is a sample activity we've used successfully in our classes as a way for students to take stock of their own work in relation to the work of their peers. Students sit in groups of three or four (more than four is usually counterproductive), seating themselves either by choice or in heterogeneous groups that we've set up. They have two class periods to complete all tasks. While the activity is not likely to work as is for any teacher, a modified version will.

Tip for success: As students complete their work, take note of their responses, but don't grade their papers. That would in large part defeat the purpose of their self- and peer assessments. However, you might like to give students a check, check-plus, or check-minus in your grade book based on your observations of how thoughtfully they attend to their work. Have students keep their responses in their portfolios for future use/reference.

Notebook/Journal/Portfolio Evaluation

Grade: 7–9
Time: One or two class periods
Outcomes: Students read, respond to, and analyze the work they've
   done in notebooks, journals, and portfolios.

Names of Others in Your Group: _____

Directions: Complete the five activities below with your group. Be sure that you engage in the process of the activities by focusing on and completing each task. Answer all questions on this evaluation sheet thoughtfully and legibly.

ACTIVITY 1: NOTEBOOK EVALUATION

1. Do you have the following entries in your own notebook? (Answer Yes or No.)
_____ The Process of Reading
_____ Foreshadowing and Irony
_____ Poe's Philosophy of Composition
_____ Literary Technique in Shirley Jackson's "The Lottery"
_____ Comma Usage in Compound Sentences
_____ Reading Aims: *Black Boy* by Richard Wright

2. Grade the above entries in two other students' notebooks, and write a brief assessment of their entries (that is, compliment them or counsel them on their spelling, neatness, completeness, dating of notes, proper capitalization of titles, and such.):

Student: _____ Grade: _____

_____

_____

Student: _____ Grade: _____

_____

_____

ACTIVITY 2: READER RESPONSE JOURNAL SHARING

Choose two entries that you would like to read aloud to your group. Once each of you has chosen two entries, take turns reading aloud to the group. Then, answer these questions:

1. Which do you like better, reading aloud or listening? Why?_____

_____

2. Are you satisfied that your group listened carefully while you read? Explain.

_____

3. Name something from or about one of the entries you heard that struck you.

_____

ACTIVITY 3: EVALUATING READER RESPONSE JOURNALS

Answer the following questions about your own journal, and then get at least one group member to validate your claims:

1. How many entries have you written in the last eight weeks? _____

2. Characterize these entries.

_____

_____

3. How many books have you read since you finished (or didn't finish) *Across Five Aprils*? _____

4. Comment upon the state of your reading. _____

_____

5. Grade your journal. _____

6. Validator's (or Validators') Signature(s): _____

ACTIVITY 4: PORTFOLIO ASSESSMENT

Read through your portfolio.

Have you included an autobiographical piece and at least one finished, polished free writing piece? _____

Share your portfolio with at least one other person in your group, and have that person write a statement of opinion about your work: _____

_____

Read all Book Cards (book reviews) your group has written. What comments do you have about them? About their reading choices?

_____

_____

ACTIVITY 5: PERSONAL STATEMENT

Write a few sentences that show self-assessment.

In other words, make two or more judgments about the state (quality) of your work so far in your notebook, journal, and portfolio—and don't forget works-in-progress from your writing folder. For example: Are you happy with your progress in English? With your progress in reading and writing? What plans do you have for your reading and writing?

_____

_____

We find that this activity and other deliberate assessments like it are an effective way for students to revisit their own work and see/hear their classmates' work. It helps them to be both interested and productive in future workshop sessions.

Student Responses to Workshop

Here's what a variety of students have to say about workshop:

EMILY: "What is workshop? A place where things are made. A reading and writing workshop, like the one I have in English, is when people write, share, revise, and edit their writing. It's also a period in which students read books and write journal entries. Workshop gives everyone an equal opportunity to express themselves. I look forward to workshop mostly because I am given a great deal of freedom of choice and I'm treated like an adult."

TIM: "The reading/writing workshop is a great idea for letting students work at their own pace. It demonstrates a low-pressure work atmosphere where I work best."

DAVE: "Ah, workshop, what a rush! I love it. You walk into English, and you're free! Free to let the ability flow from your mind onto the paper, as I am doing now. Free from the bonds of teachers, so you can teach yourself."

DAVID: "Workshop is unique. It's the only class that gives us a chance to discover answers without the usual teacher interjections, which can really annoy you: 'I'll give you a clue . . . it has to do with . . . it starts with an M . . . I'll just tell you myself because I always see the same hands . . .' "

TARA: "Workshop really is a class act. It's a way of extending your feelings to the people who surround your hard desk—the desk that makes your elbows dirty. From these extensions start seeds that germinate into creative pieces of writing. I'll always remember this class. We depend on each other."

DANA: "Workshop was a new experience for me this year. It gave me the opportunity to write my feelings and thoughts on paper, thoughts that I probably would not have written at home. The quiet enabled me to concentrate on what I was doing, I was drawn into my writing. Many times I was in a world of my own; what I wrote, I lived. When this happened, it totally relaxed me. It made me enjoy writing. I came up with short pieces, serious writings, humorous adventures, poems, and wrote what came into my head."

What these students say about their experiences with workshop underscores some of its basic premises:

- Students look forward to regular, predictable times for reading and writing in school.
- Students appreciate choices of topic, genre, pacing, and process.
- Students value responses (especially from each other) while reading and writing is happening.

As well, this sampling of responses implies what a workshop is not:

- License to take it easy or to do no work
- A perfect configuration
- A disorganized or noisy free-for-all
- An automatic "A" (few students mention grades when they discuss workshop)

Alternative Activity: Read Around—Choose a Piece of Your Own Writing

Grade: 7–12
Time: One class period
Outcome: Students read and share a piece of their own writing; students hear each other's voices and see themselves as part of a writing community

We use this activity at least once each semester when we join English and social studies classes. It's an excellent alternative to the typical or traditional oral report, which may be too formal or inappropriate or lengthy an assignment to weave into workshop classes. We bring a podium into our classroom, and students read to an audience of about fifty.

Important note: The podium brings seriousness to the task, but we keep the assignment simple, and we downplay the experience. We don't use a rubric—no ten points for poise or ten for looking up. We give students only a day or two to choose a piece to read—the less time for them to be nervous, the better. We want a sharing of each other's voices in writing—a respectful and positive speaking and listening experience.

Here's the activity: Choose a piece of your own writing to read aloud and share with the class (free writing, autobiographical sketch, social studies journal entry, reader response, poem, etc.):

1. Step up to the podium and greet your audience. (perhaps "Good morning, class" or "Hello, everyone")
2. Tell your audience what you have chosen to read (and why you've chosen it, if you want).
3. Read the piece aloud.
4. Thank your audience.

Speak clearly and deliberately, not too fast.

Here's one student's response to this read aloud alternative:

"I was really surprised by the reaction I got from my reading. I didn't expect so many people would think it was funny, and when people were saying it was their favorite piece, it made me feel good. I think it increased my confidence in speaking in front of a large group of people.

I know the last time we did this, I was a nervous wreck. My hand was shaking so much I could barely hold the paper. But the best part is when you step away from the podium, everyone's clapping for you, and you realize you did it. It was no big deal for a lot of people, and I have to hand it to them for being so relaxed, but for me it was like hitting a home run.

I remember in fourth grade I had to give an oral presentation about Harry Houdini. I got halfway through his life, and then my mouth slammed shut. Totally blank, the lights went out. My palms were wet, my throat became dry and sore. I slowly walked back to my seat. I wanted to cry, but I held it in. I felt as if I were going to explode, just scream out loud, but I didn't. Since then, I've never been the same, but this helped me out a lot.

6
Voice Is Vision

"Tell all the Truth but tell it slant / Success in Circuit lies."
—*Emily Dickinson*

We'd like to encourage writing teachers to begin instruction with an emphasis on personal, expressive writing—it's the best way for students to take control of their writing. Initially, students who write about ideas, situations, or subjects that they know about naturally are motivated to express themselves. They possess the credentials—knowledge, feeling, experience, words—to write about personal subjects, and so the process works more smoothly and ultimately may produce better results than if they write initially on unfamiliar subjects. Students can find their voice in expressive writing and evolve from an informal stance to a more formal one. Furthermore, we should admit to students that most good formal writing also maintains some degree of personal voice.

A recurring line teachers hear from students in a writing classroom is "I know what I want to say, but I just don't know how to write it." Or "I have the ideas in my head, but I have a hard time putting them on paper."

A common misconception in teaching writing is that we need to assign student writers ideas or topics. Listen to what students are saying: often they *do* know what they want to write about, but they can't decide how to best express their feelings or ideas. They have difficulty in formulating an approach to expressing their thoughts. Spend time on developing and practicing a variety of effective methods to express thoughts. Show examples and let students practice them, so they begin to see writing in new ways. They'll begin to recognize writing techniques as they read. They'll learn what works. If we can stimulate a need to write, rather than focus on an externally applied pressure to write, we may unlock a writer.

We'd like to offer an alternative approach, along the lines of what Emily Dickinson suggests, that emphasizes a personal stance. What gives students power or control over their own writing is not an inordinate concentration on *what* they are writing; it's more productive to focus on *how* they decide to express their thoughts. Assist them with definite ways to write what they want to share. Telling their ideas "slant" or in a personal way can cause readers to feel what they feel. Let students generate many possibilities to write about, and then give them options to express these thoughts.

Dispel the notion that if writers organize their thoughts sequentially, use standard transitions, and inform their readers about a topic, it will result in a good piece of writing. A detailed outline doesn't always help students figure out how to best write their thoughts. The lockstep approach—the orderly movement from A to Z—doesn't always lead to success. The direct approach, fine for directions, for delivering facts and many forms of informative writing, may be less effective when the purpose is to move readers emotionally or to engage them on other intellectual levels (see Chapter 3 and Bloom's Taxonomy). We want students to aim for this visceral reaction to their writing.

How can we improve students' skill in expressing thoughts? First, we must ask students to examine good writing and the ways writers reveal their thoughts. We can note a writer's purpose. Before writing about a selected topic, student writers should answer these questions:

- How will you help your reader see, feel, or understand what you are writing about?
- How can you open your piece to capture and maintain your readers' attention?
- What words can you use to specifically show what you mean?
- How will you close your piece? What lasting effect do you want to leave?

Students may have difficulty answering these prewriting questions. At first, expect mixed reactions or confused responses to these questions. Students aren't accustomed to teachers asking them to state their purpose in writing or how they expect to achieve their result. *Our advice*: don't give in and allow them to disregard this critical stage. Yes, the purpose and expectations can change during writing, but it's critical to have some notion of these before and during the act. Eventually, students who can respond to questions about their writing develop a necessary control over their writing; additionally, it gives us a place to begin instruction. When students make personal decisions about their writing, they will focus on *how* and not just *what* they're writing. This effort produces better writing and more satisfied writers.

In the following student example, you can see the effect of this approach. First, Dawn answered the four prewriting intention questions; then, she wrote her piece; finally, she reviewed her intentions and made appropriate revisions to produce a finished piece. Here are the prewriting questions and her answers:

My Purpose in Writing

How will you help your reader see, feel, or understand what you are writing about?

I know that readers think death is a terrible thing, but I want people to look past the physical loss. I want to tell about my mother, and by relating my experience, give some comfort to others who have suffered the death of a loved one. I want to describe specific points I remember about my mother and my feelings in the hospital when she died. I want to contrast what others may think is typical to what I really felt.

How can you open your piece to capture and maintain your readers' attention?

I want to focus on a positive picture of my mother and what an outstanding person she was. I want to set readers up and give them a surprise when they find out the most important gift she gave me is the one I got on her deathbed.

What words can you use to specifically show what you mean?

Words about my mom: unquenchable, plague, limitations
Words about the experience: tranquillity, hint, promise, hope
Words about the hospital: solemn, sterile, glimmer, sunshine

How will you close your piece? What lasting effect do you want to leave?

I want to end with the idea that this experience helps me now. I want readers to have a good feeling about what my mother did. I want readers to have a different feeling about death and the mystery of life.

Here is the personal essay Dawn wrote:

THE GIFT OF HOPE

Before she left, my mother gave me many gifts. She provided me with a warm, secure home in which to develop and explore as a child. She taught me to read, and patiently answered my every question, bestowing upon me an unquenchable desire to learn. She told me of legends and myths that encouraged the wild stories of my youth. She unlocked my imagination. My mother taught me about nature so I would have respect for, not fear, all of God's creatures. She helped me accept many types of people, so I would not grow up prejudiced or be deceived by appearances. And my mother would always go out of her way to give a compliment or do a favor for someone because she taught me that a person should do a "good deed" each day and take pleasure in making other people smile.

My mother gave me many gifts, but she gave me the most important gift of all on the day she died. Our family had gathered into the small hospital room, where a feeling of solemnity prevailed. We knew it was time. My mother's breathing had become slow and shallow, as if each expansion of her lungs was a pure act of will. Her emaciated body seemed now only a shell, a fake imitation of life. The worst had come, yet we felt more relief than anything. Carol Williams would finally be out of the pain that had plagued her for so long. No more doctors and needles, no more weakness and limitations. There was a sense of fading in the room, and there amidst the harsh, sterile glare of hospital equipment and the comfort of her forever loving and devoted family, my mother passed away. Then, something extraordinary happened. Throughout my mother's last weeks alive, I had held back tears. I had to be strong for my mother. But at that moment, I felt no urge to cry; I felt my mother go. It was an odd feeling, and I was overcome by a great sense of peace. I felt that I had been living in a dim, cramped room, and upon leaving, my mother opened the door and let in a glimmer of bright sunshine on the other side. My mother, even as she left this world, thought of me. She gave me a hint, a promise, of what life is all about.

Now, in times of doubt or loneliness, I have only to think of that one moment, and I have nothing to fear. Whenever I think of my mother, and grief is so hard on me at times that I feel my heart will burst, I think of where she is now and the tranquillity I felt as she left, and all my troubles melt away. Even on her deathbed, my mother never stopped giving. That day, she gave me the gift of hope.

Dawn's ability to articulate her purpose helped produce this writing. With clear intentions, she felt more comfortable in writing the first draft. She had freedom to deviate from her plan, but the structure guided her. Let students establish their purposes, write their pieces, and review their intentions. This analysis produces a more confident writer, one who has control.

Tip for success: Whenever we provide structure or a plan to help students, we must couch it in a way that does not limit their creativity, voice, or common sense. We must keep alive the possibility for surprise, an unexpected twist, or a new angle to occur during the writing. Tell students to be alert for this.

Weaving Text

A useful technique for students to practice and develop is the ability to weave text quoted from other sources into their own writing. Gaining competence with this skill transfers to other disciplines in which writing must contain integrated text. Formal research writing and persuasive writing require the ability to support ideas with credible evidence taken from reputable sources. Students should see how carefully selected text-bytes can strengthen their writing.

The craft of using quoted bits of text successfully requires that students become adept at three specific skills:

- Selecting relevant text or useful quotations
- Cutting the text appropriately
- Weaving the text so it blends smoothly into their writing

Students need to see examples of these distinct skills; they will need to practice selecting, cutting, and weaving to gain facility and confidence. Once students understand and practice weaving text, they possess a valuable writing tool.

Tip for success: Many students are able to choose a quotation that relates to a topic or point they may be writing about. There's more to it. It is the masterful weaving or blending of the selected text-byte that maintains the rhythm of a sentence. Typically students write a sentence using quoted text and a follow-up that look like this:

> Award-winning author Thomas Gray stated, "A well-chosen verb makes all the difference in good writing." This is a good point to consider for a writer.

The text-byte selection is a good one, yet these two separate sentences together lack voice and interest. Admittedly, the first sentence shows evidence of weaving in the quoted line, yet students can accomplish this weave or blend more skillfully and with better results. Show students ways to connect these sentences to flow more naturally or seamlessly. Here are two revisions in which students have blended the quoted text into their own sentences:

> Award-winning author Thomas Gray reminds writers to consider a "well-chosen verb" because this "makes all the difference in good writing."

> or an alternative sentence

> Concerned writers agree with Thomas Gray's belief that a "well-chosen verb makes all the difference in good writing."

The first place to focus students' attention is on the word(s) leading into the quoted text, often the sticking point for effective text-weaving. Discuss the sound of the revised sentences. Read them aloud to hear the rhythm.

To weave text effectively, students should answer these three questions and make choices:

- What distinctive word(s) in the selected text should I use?
- What word(s) support the point I'm trying to make?
- What word(s) can I omit?

Tip for success: Skill in text weaving takes practice—a lot of trial and error. Encourage students to find and share excellent examples of this technique. Use news articles, textbooks, or magazines that weave quoted text. Let students examine how the sentences work, what makes them flow, how they're punctuated, and how the text blends in with the writer's voice. Eventually students see how good writers use text-bytes effectively, to give their points power.

A good way to demonstrate selecting, cutting, and weaving is to use a poem or short piece of prose as a source for students. By using a brief common source to generate sentences, students can compare choices and techniques.

For example, we can use Rick Alley's poem "Tomato" as a source for writing sentences that incorporate quoted text. You can share the student samples that follow the poem.

> TOMATO
>
> August is a machine, one I sometimes
> taste. Life at a glance, a garter snake
>
> scribbles away from a cat. Time to let
> the garden riot, the truant vines
>
> go wild. To the cat in the weeds' ancient shade,
> I'm not even here in my yard.
>
> once I thought the sun made noise, code
> for the drying grass. Now I know
>
> heat begins with the junebug's
> high vibrato. August is machine,
>
> but a tender one with gears: a junebug flipped
> on its rounded back,
>
> working panicky legs.

The following samples illustrate ways students use text and alternative ways to weave quoted text:

Sample 1

Original: The poet states that "Now I know heat begins with the junebug's high vibrato."

Alternative: The speaker realizes that the summer's "heat begins with the junebug's high vibrato."

The original sentence states a fact from the poem. The alternative example refers to the "speaker" in the poem, cuts the quoted text, and blends it into a sentence that includes commentary.

Sample 2

Original: In the summer the poem describes "the garden riot, the truant vines/go wild."

Alternative: Readers understand why the speaker "let the garden riot," and doesn't care if "the truant vines/go wild" in August.

Again, the original sentence uses the quoted text simply to state a fact in the poem. The alternative sentence blends the text into the sentence and makes an assertion.

Sample 3

Original: Rick Alley's poem "Tomato" states that "August is a machine."

Alternative: In Rick Alley's poem "Tomato," the image that "August is a machine" helps readers understand the power of August.

Once again, the original sentence merely states a fact using a line from the poem. The alternative sentence adds the writer's interpretation of the selected text.

The handout shown in Figure 6–1 provides useful practice for students in text-weaving. Expect several effective versions and share decisions that work.

Ways to Open

Students must master a variety of techniques for writing an opening. Students need to know that openings depend on the purpose and audience for a particular piece of writing, but we can agree on several basic aims for *all* openings:

ALL OPENINGS SHOULD

- Create interest
- State the subject clearly
- Give the writer's point of view

Using selected quoted text in your writing is a skill that you can master with practice. Weaving text or blending quoted text into your writing is a technique that you will use often in a variety of writing assignments.

Revise the following samples to practice weaving text effectively. You will need to select, cut, and weave text into a sentence that makes an assertion. The text supports the point you want to make.

Avoid introducing text with *said*. Write your revisions on another sheet of paper.

1. Charlie Chaplin gave people the opportunity to laugh in a world when there were difficult times. He once said, "In the end, everything is a gag." This quotation describes his life in many ways.

2. Harry Houdini is still known as the best escape artist who ever lived. All of his escapes test his courage and persistence. Houdini's famous and favorite quote was, "When I clap my hands three times, behold a miracle."

3. When Rosa Parks refused to move to the back of the bus, the driver threatened to call the police. She said to him, "Go ahead and call them."

4. Margaret Thatcher resigned in 1990. "Democracy isn't just about deducing what people want. Democracy is leading the people as well." Thatcher had a great impact on society and did a good job as a leader.

5. Before going on his shuttle mission, John Glenn made a comment about where his personal influence came from. "Right now there are some thirty-five million Americans over the age of sixty-five. I view myself as representing those people in my effort in space flight."

FIGURE 6–1. Integrating quotations effectively

Since we suggest that good writing initially comes from a personal and expressive stance, the most important of these criteria initially is creating an interest in your readers to read on.

It's necessary to show students examples of openings (collect and use models from every source possible). Get students to recognize good openings (from a single sentence to a paragraph or several paragraphs in some cases); get them to discuss how they work; encourage them to bring openings into class and to share them; have them model these openings in their own pieces.

Ask a student to write several different openings for the same piece and to decide on one. Let the class discuss the writer's choices for openings. Here are five effective ways (with samples) to open a piece:

1. Striking Statement: This makes a reader take notice for a number of reasons—a provocative word, a personal revelation, an unusual stance.

   Sample: *I lead a life that no one else can say she's led.*

2. Incongruent Statement: This appears to be unrelated to the piece itself, but has a useful connection seen and revealed by the writer; an unusual, personal or tangential relation grabs the reader's attention.

   Sample: *Dark clouds, lightning, and a torrential downpour are no cause for alarm for a group of meteorologists in training. These natural occurrences provide an excellent opportunity to study weather patterns.*

3. Quoted Text Weave: This makes use of two interesting bits of a quotation that sets ups a contrast or contradiction that the reader detects between sports and music; a few well-chosen words or striking phrase make the reader take note.

   Sample: *Wendy, record-breaking scorer for the Wildcats, admits that she "never intended to play high school field hockey" because she'd rather spend time pursuing her "passion for playing the piano."*

4. Leading Anecdote: This uses a short narrative clip that naturally draws a reader into a piece; a story captures a reader who wants to find out where it's going or how it ends.

   Sample: *After a fourteen-hour flight, Jason emerged from the plane fatigued and disoriented. His first impression of this strange country began with a blast of dank air and the sound of hundreds of birds in the trees surrounding the airfield. He wondered about his decision to volunteer in a place like this.*

5. Direct Address: This is an intentionally direct statement aimed at a reader; this challenges readers (individually and collectively) to get involved in the piece by questioning, accepting, or inquiring further about the writer's statement.

Sample: *The next time you shut off the lights late at night to go to bed, think about Cara Davis, whose routine workday is about to begin. While we sleep in the comfort of our beds, she methodically collects data to make our life easier.*

Just Say Something

After we work on openings, we have to attack the rest of the piece. When we ask students to write for themselves or for a particular audience, we guide them with this suggestion: *Readers will excuse a slightly flawed performance if you say something worth reading.* Saying something noteworthy is the quality we expect any piece of writing, initially and ultimately, to possess. Without an element of brilliance or revelation, writing dies on the vine.

We must assist students to root out this quality (if it exists, and often it does) lying amidst uninspired words, before the piece enters the final drafting stage or becomes a public piece. Readers tire quickly when writing says little or doesn't move them. It's essential to communicate this to student writers. An element of revelation, even in its roughest state, supersedes correctness and form. We need to look for it and invite it in a student piece; it's worth the effort.

Recently, a colleague of ours who teaches geography complained about the "uninspired writing" on papers he had received from his students. (He figured English teachers could provide some solace.) His assignment was an excellent one: he had asked his students to read any book of their choice and discuss concepts from the text through the eyes of a geographer. He gave them several geographical categories from which they could choose to apply the particulars of their selected books.

The assignment had structure, a real purpose, and offered wide choices for students; and it was not overly prescriptive. It asked students to adopt the persona of a geographer and use this perspective to see and describe the world. What better way to learn about geography and its impact than to become a geographer? Here was a teacher who had constructed an interesting assignment and made good on the effort to involve his students actively in their subject. Yet the results were disappointing, and he wondered why.

We reviewed the stack of papers and discovered intensive written comments concerning style, corrective marks on mechanics filling the margins, and many instances where he had edited poor writing he found. As we leafed through the pile, we saw what troubled this teacher. It wasn't only the lack of mechanical correctness that had gotten him so frustrated, although this is what ultimately became his focus judging by the comments he had written on the papers. It was the absence of genuine thought and personal insight, but he had little experience in composing and sharing these kinds of comments.

Many of these students had written glorified book reports (according to him)—little more than summaries of the books with scattered obligatory references to geography, usually coming in the form of description of the physical setting. They assumed this would satisfy what they thought was the intent of the assignment. We noticed that some had demonstrated acceptable standards for correctness (despite the teacher's first impression, there were a considerable number of these); still, what irked the teacher was that most of these writers had written little of value. Instead, they had skimmed the surface of geography, throwing in a few catch phrases now and then, to make it appear that they had adopted a heightened perspective.

Before launching into a diatribe on the writing process, we thought carefully about how we could and should respond. Here was a teacher who wanted help. We offered the following advice:

1. First, skip the corrective mechanical comments and the need to assign a final grade to each paper. Return papers that say little; don't let students off the hook with a bad grade; it's *not* about grades. Take a quick look at the papers, and in some cases, return them for recasting or polishing. Spend time in class on specific ideas that make writing about geography effective. Collect and share a few good examples that work.

2. Don't spend hours reading, revising, or editing papers that are marred by surface errors. Break down the overwhelming task of revising by having students start by recasting sentences and paragraphs that have some value. Use these few good samples to encourage students to continue revising longer sections of the paper.

3. Provoke, question, or probe students so that they'll write about their books with more depth; tell them to abandon the book report persona—to act, see, and speak like a geographer. More questions about specific concepts and interesting parts of the paper will inspire more writing.

We further reviewed the papers and suggested some changes in the type of comments he wrote that might create anger or confusion in students. We culled a few papers for individual conferencing with him.

The teacher tried some of our suggestions. He gave students an opportunity to write again. Were the revised papers successful? In many cases, they were. For those students who missed the mark (the second time as well), the suggestions moved them a bit closer to success. The teacher accepted the notion that the process for this first paper needed attention so that an acceptable paper would result. We expect (and this is always hopeful) that future papers may need less time from the beginning of the process to reach the final product.

Here are two sample paragraphs of pieces improved through revision. Both are first-person accounts of the effect of a place on an individual, one of the specific geographical categories from the original assignment:

> I was awestruck by the magnificence of the Colorado mountains. The blazing sunsets there are unimaginable. When the sun sets a brilliant palette of colors paints the mountains and clouds around Boulder. It's majestic and moving. Sometimes, just after the sun disappears behind the distant peaks, the light radiates and encircles everything, making it difficult to determine which way is west. This is the Colorado I discovered and love.
>
> Jeremy

In this next opening, the writer communicates an emotional attachment he feels to a place he loves.

> My favorite place to travel on Virginia's Eastern Shore is along the back roads that head north along the Atlantic and Chesapeake Bay. These bayside roads were once horse and wagon trails that still meander haphazardly, passing through quaint little villages that once served as ports for watermen on the bay. The Seaside Road, a turtle back road, narrow and consisting of coarse stones, begins near the tip of the peninsula at Cape Charles. This road reveals the true Eastern Shore, the way it was and the way it is.
>
> Preston

Tip for success: We reaffirmed with this teacher that revision neither implies failure nor a lowering of standards—a feeling he had harbored. If the goal is to get good writing, sometimes even brilliant writing, then we should do whatever it takes. We don't let students get away with misguided attempts or missed opportunities if we feel that something more can come from another attempt. We should focus on the work and how to get the best out of our students; after that, it is up to them.

Always Be Closing

Another problem students face is how to end a piece of writing. We know how students too often end a piece: they just stop writing. What choices do students make to close a piece? If they've listened to what writing teachers have told them, they may do one of two things: (1) restate the thesis or topic sentence or (2) summarize the main point(s) of the piece.

Rather than limit students to these standard closings, we should provide several options for closing. Readers remember closings that do more than merely repeat ideas or reword the thesis. We should expect a closing to interest and move a reader as much as an opening.

What works? The most effective closing doesn't formally announce the upcoming conclusion. Readers tire of markers that state "And in conclusion . . ." or "Finally, I would like to close by saying . . ." or any variation of these announcements. Encourage writers to compose an ending that results in one of these conditions:

- It reveals a change in view.
- It presents a poignant idea.
- It shows a significant reflection, leaving readers with a lasting impression.

Here are four closings that end with power. The first two examples are based on photographs that the writers used as prompts. The first sample leaves us with an enduring image.

> My grandfather deserved to suffer less, and the end did mercifully arrive. Now when I visit his house, I feel only his spirit there. I press my hot, tear-stained face to the cool glass frame of his photograph on the wall to hear his comforting voice, to hear his stories one more time.
>
> Pete

In Casey's essay, she writes about a home where she once lived. She uses her imagination to recall this faint childhood memory.

> For many years, the memory of that wonderful place has been submerged, lost in time. Now thanks to a faded photograph, it has returned—intact and beautiful—and I will cherish it by returning to that scene again and again in my thoughts. The wild violets lining the path to our house are not as vibrant in the photo as they must have been twelve years ago. But for me, they continue to be as colorful as they once were.
>
> Casey

Patrick's essay describes a painful relationship with his father. He closes his reflective piece by revealing how his past has influenced him.

> For years I was reclusive, trying to find what I once lost, trying to tell myself that I was not like my father. This took some time. By no means am I forgiving him for all that he did, but I understand what he did. I didn't like his behavior then, and I still can't condone it today. Although he lives on in my memory, he will never gain my approval.
>
> Patrick

And finally, Jennifer ends her essay with a significant point—how she and her family resisted the influence of a neighborhood where they once lived.

> We lived on Bay Street for a while, but this place did not get to live in us. Bay Street did not take root within anyone I loved. Not even, in the end, with my mother.
>
> Jennifer

Tip for success. In these personal and expressive pieces, each writer chose to share meaningful recollections and thoughts. When writers describe people, places, and events in their lives, readers should be moved by strong images and connections. This is what such a closing should do.

Alternative Activity: Mechanics Mania

Once students have written a piece that has meaning, this activity allows them to use their own writing and revise their own sentences (these can be mechanical or stylistic revisions). Encourage students to make this an ongoing activity. Assign several samples to be turned in periodically, share useful examples, and include the best samples as a part of a writing portfolio. Encourage students to use grammar handbooks, the Internet, and other appropriate texts as sources for their revisions. Students can revise a bland opening or closing or experiment with several possible revisions.

> **Grade:** 9–12
> **Time:** Ongoing homework assignment
> **Outcome:** To improve revision using personal writing samples

Mechanics Mania
Compile a journal of personal mechanical or stylistic concerns that need revision in your writing. Each entry should be titled and contain three parts:

1. The original sentence or sample as it was written
2. The revised work (one or *more* ways to make it right)
3. A personalized written rule or explanation for the revision

Your journal should reflect a variety of mechanical/technical revisions from your papers. You can record two samples on each page. Consider several ways to resolve the problem. *Highlight* the revised sentence(s). Here's a sample entry:

TITLE: COMBINING TWO THOUGHTS

1. He staggered out of the gym and he collapsed on the sidewalk.
2. A. *He staggered out of the gym, and he collapsed on the sidewalk.*
   B. *Staggering out of the gym, he collapsed on the sidewalk.*
3. When joining two complete thoughts with *and* (a conjunction), I need to put a comma before the and. I can begin a sentence with a phrase followed by a comma.

Here's another sample entry:

WORD CHOICE

1. The play concerns itself mostly with how a family adheres together to survive.
2. A. *The family members in this play cling to each other to survive.*
   B. *The play reveals how a family can survive by staying together.*
3. I can edit unnecessary words and revise others to write a better sentence.

Voice in writing and the freedom to express it can unlock hidden thoughts and insights in students. Success and facility with personal expressive writing creates an easier transition to more formal writing. We've seen it over and over. Unlock imagination, emotion, memories and the mind pours out ideas that can be used as a starting point for all writing tasks.

7

Heterogeneous Grouping
Reading and Writing Across Tracks and Disciplines

Heterogeneously grouped classes mix students of all ability levels into one classroom: high, middle, and low achievers are all represented. In a truly heterogeneous grouping, no one group—such as honors or remedial—has been taken from the mix and grouped homogeneously.

The teacher's challenge is to use methods that will enable all students to engage in curriculum, without limiting more capable students or alienating less capable ones. This chapter contains such methods, suggestions, and models for teachers who want to bring interdisciplinary lesson planning and learning into heterogeneously grouped classrooms.

Creating Effective Heterogeneous Classrooms

The following suggestions are useful for creating effective lessons and learning experiences for students across tracks and disciplines:

1. Instruct the class at large before students work in groups. Consider the following activities: reading aloud a short poem, essay, or story; introducing what students will be expected to do; conducting a question and answer session about a given topic; guided free writing; demonstrating a structure or a skill; conducting a survey or experiment.
2. Mix the kinds of reading the students do: selections should vary in genre, style, origin, and difficulty level. Choose and offer both simple pieces and challenging pieces to show students that there is no one required level of writing or reading for any class.
3. Examine the process of reading with students as you help them to make reading habitual; help them to learn and feel what successful readers do: decode, visualize, pay attention to new or unfamiliar

words, make predictions, make connections and comparisons, self-question, search for information, check comprehension, confirm/reject previous assumptions or predictions, draw conclusions.

4. Group students in different ways: Groups should not be permanently singular. Students should not have to work with the same three classmates for an entire year. Some teachers divide the class heterogeneously into *home* groups or *base* groups early in the school year. Students work in other pairs or groups as the year goes on, but for selected activities, especially as units of study begin and end, students return periodically to their base groups. This practice can provide stability and encourage growth all at once. Note these configurations as well:

- Sometimes, form heterogeneous groups (four students per group is optimal) so that students interact with classmates they might not otherwise acknowledge.
- Other times, allow students to choose their own groups—for example, when you want students to edit a personal piece of writing with a partner or with classmates they feel comfortable with.
- Have students do group work casually at times, allowing cooperation and collaboration to occur naturally; help groups that need guidance.
- Use cooperative models such as those advocated by D. W. Johnson, et al. in *Cooperation in the Classroom* (1991). One such model is the jigsaw, where students divide the given task into equal parts. Each student then researches and becomes an expert on one of the parts, sometimes by joining classmates from other cooperative groups who are working on the same part of the "puzzle" as they are. Each returns to the base group and teaches the information he's gathered and learned to the other group members. Generally, a quiz of some sort follows.
- Allow students to work in pairs, especially when one can teach or quiz another on a concrete topic, such as mastering spelling or vocabulary words.

5. Plan lessons that enable students to learn in different ways: by using listening (to music or to a piece being read aloud) as the core of the lesson; by creating a simple project or work of art; through traditionally academic reading and writing assignments, and so on.

6. Maintain a clear organization for the classroom, but know that students learn in subtle ways—socially, haphazardly, and unpredictably.

7. Use a variety of methods of assessment, including keeping, developing, and assessing a portfolio for use in a final portfolio project. Don't get overwhelmed with study questions, tests, quizzes, or homework—use them evenly and purposefully. For example, don't assign study questions every night for homework.

8. Aim for assignments to be open-ended, achievable by all students but not so simple as to constrict or bore capable students: simple in set-up, but not in concept or in possibilities.

9. Accomplish traditional aims through cooperative, collaborative group activities. Involve students in processes that will engage them in both academic tasks and challenges and face-to-face interaction. Create opportunities where students have both choice and responsibility as they take on significant academic tasks in a cooperative group setting.

10. Have students create simple, on-the-spot visuals for the assignments they do.

Literature Circles

Grade: 7–12

Time: Ongoing; one week of lessons for teaching students what literature circles are and engaging them in a literature circle in response to a short work

Outcome: Each group of students directs and synthesizes its reading assignment; they summarize, discuss, illustrate, and elicit and explicate quotes from their reading.

For years, English teachers have put students into groups and assigned each group a different novel to read, sometimes a selection of different titles related to a common theme. Students are grouped by their own interests and choices or by teacher design, and they are asked to carry out different tasks, often including mastering vocabulary, answering questions, discussing the reading, tracing character growth and development, identifying theme, and giving oral presentations.

Sometimes such groupings work well—unless the teacher feels responsible for too many books at once, taking on responsibility for reading each book and guiding each group through the reading. Or, the teacher may feel like some students are not contributing fairly to the group, leaving a group's work to one or two students. If a teacher feels thus burdened or limited by his role in guiding groups, his stance will be negative and the group work will not succeed.

Literature circles offer an excellent opportunity for students in heterogeneous groups to take on different roles and responsibilities as they read and examine a work of literature together. Teachers can use Harvey Daniels' *Literature Circles: Voice and Choice in the Student-Centered Classroom* (1994) as the basis for the concept. As well, an Internet search will yield valuable information. Teachers will be able to coordinate an effective reading experience for students in all classes.

Creating a literature circle experience for students exemplifies what good teachers do:

- They inform their teaching through reading and research.
- They model their own teaching on the successful practices of others.
- They modify those practices to suit their own needs without sacrificing the essence of the practiced structure or proven method.

In literature circles, students can read and study books of their own common choice and interest, or a teacher may choose students' books. In either case, the teacher creates literature circles to involve heterogeneous groups of four all reading the same work.

Recently, a student teacher of ours decided to create literature circles in English 8. Given a selection of works from which to choose, he considered John Steinbeck's *The Pearl* a good choice: not too long, of literary merit, and of mixed appeal. He also decided that preceding study of *The Pearl*, groups should have a trial run of sorts with literature circles, for which he chose "On the Brink," a Cynthia Rylant short story.

To introduce literature circles to our classes, we developed a set of notes to discuss with the students. In doing so, we discussed the roles suggested by Harvey Daniels and decided to modify some of them. As well, we decided to include procedural information for students: we designed our literature circles experience to complement an established curriculum and reading/writing workshop structure. We discussed the following notes with students:

1. What are literature circles? They are reading and discussion groups where each member takes on specific roles and responsibilities for each day of discussion.
2. How are literature circles set up? We (your teachers) will form mixed groups of students, four (or five, if necessary) students per group. Each group member will have a specific role for each reading assignment. These roles will rotate with each new assignment.
3. What are the roles?

- Summarizer: This person gives a brief overview of the reading assignment to show the main ideas and highlight key points. (*Note:* For a relatively simple book, this role is likewise simple. For a challenging reading assignment, paraphrasing the reading or offering a synopsis of key points is a more complex task.)
- Discussion Starter/Director: This person is responsible for starting the discussion, getting all members of the group to contribute, and leading the discussion using a list of questions that focus on major ideas or points from the reading.
- Passage Finder: This person locates important or interesting passages to share and discuss with the group. The passage finder also locates interesting or unfamiliar words and phrases to discuss.
- Illustrator: This person draws a sketch—some kind of picture or graphic representation influenced by the reading. The illustrator should not show the picture until the discussion director calls for it. Then, the group discusses the picture rather than the illustrator explaining it.
- Investigator/Connector (for groups with five members): This person finds background or related information for the book; she makes connections between the book and the world beyond it.

4. How often will we have literature circles? We will have four literature circles for our reading of *The Pearl*; thereafter, sessions may be fewer or greater in number, depending on the work being read and studied.

5. How will a literature circles class be organized?
- Class begins, the teacher asks students to respond to a question or two; students keep responses in folders set up for literature circles (quick-write—five to eight minutes).
- In each group, the summarizer gives key points of the reading (two–three minutes).
- The discussion director of each group starts and leads the discussion by using prepared questions and by calling on passage finders, illustrators, and connectors to carry out their roles (twenty to twenty-five minutes).
- The teacher concludes the lesson with the whole class: discussion, quick-write assessment, etc. (five to eight minutes).

We set up a separate folder for each student; this helped to keep literature circle papers and activities organized. As well, we set up response forms for students to fill out for each assigned role. We had decided that for a six-chapter book like *The Pearl*, two literary circles a week for two weeks would afford enough time for a valuable experience without risking overkill. As well, since our students were accustomed to working cooperatively and independently in a workshop setting, we preceded these four sessions with one explanation and demonstration: notes and discussion for the first session, and the "practice" run-through using the Cynthia Rylant story for the second. We had already chosen heterogeneous groups of students, which we shared with students right after notes and discussion—just before we tried literature circles with the short story.

We were pleased with how literature circles unfolded in our classes; students were prepared to carry out their roles, and they engaged in the process the way we asked them to. Our experiences with literature circles parallel other teaching experiences—like the ones we've had with reading/writing workshops—where less specific teacher direction results in questioning and learning that a more traditional method of presentation might not yield. For example, note these questions that one student prepared for her role as discussion director. Her questions are varied, thought-provoking, and academic, if not as sophisticated as a capable teacher might write. Furthermore, her group members answered more questions in greater depth than they might have had the teacher herself assigned those same questions as individual classwork or homework:

1. In the end of Chapter 4, who do you think hurt Kino?
2. What do you think of the pearl merchants? Do you think Kino was cheated?
3. How come John Steinbeck doesn't reveal who put the hole in Kino's boat or who burned their house down?
4. How did Coyotito get killed?
5. Why do you think Kino and Juana let everyone believe they are dead?
6. What did you think of the ending? The book? What did you like/dislike?
7. Why do you think Kino and Juana walked side by side at the end, when they walked into town?
8. How did Juana feel having her son die in her arms? How did you feel when Coyotito died?
9. What do you think was going through Kino and Juana's heads when they re-entered the village at the end? Do you think they were thinking the same thing?
10. How would you have ended the book?

It's okay for discussion directors to write fewer than ten or twenty questions; in fact, Harvey Daniels' book and other sources offer templates for each role—and these templates generally have four to six blanks for each category.

Figures 7–1, 7–2, and 7–3 show these student responses to our own version of such templates. It's easy to design templates to your own specifications, and they work well in keeping students on target as roles change with each literature circle.

Summarizer

Name   _Chris R._   Group _2_

Book _THE PEARL_

Meeting Date   _3/12/_

Assignment: Pages _41_ to _90_

<u>Summarizer</u>: Your job is to write a brief synopsis of today's reading assignment to start

your group discussion. Focus on key points and events.

<u>Summary</u>:

> Kino learns from the pearl merchants that the pearl is worthless, but he doesn't trust them & decides to try to sell it at the capitol. The next morning, Kino awakens & finds Juana about to throw the pearl away. So, he hits her and takes the pearl back. Then he is attacked by an unknown attacker. Kino kills the attacker. He and his family flee the city.

<u>Key Points</u>:

1. Kino kills his attacker.
2. Kino's house and canoe are destroyed.
3. Kino is hunted by trackers.
4. Kino & Juana return to La Paz with a dead Coyotito
5. Kino throws the pearl into the sea

<u>Connections</u>: What did today's reading remind you of?

> It reminded me of the movie _The Fugitive_ because after Kino kills his attacker, he goes on the run.

FIGURE 7–1. Summarizer sheet

Discussion Starter/Leader

Name __Chris R.__   Group __2__

Book __The Pearl__

Meeting Date __Feb. 27__

Assignment: Pages __1__ to __20__

<u>Discussion Starter/Leader</u>: Your job is an important one: First, you need to develop a list of questions for your group to discuss. Base your questions on issues that you find interesting and important and that you think are worthy of discussion. You'll use some/all of these questions to start and lead your discussion. Second, you will monitor the discussion so that you have enough time to call upon the passage finder and the illustrator to share their work.

<u>Discussion Questions/Topics</u>:

1. What is your favorite part? Why?
2. So far, which character do you find most interesting?
3. What do you think of the doctor's actions? Why?
4. How would you describe the author's writing style?
5. How do you think the pearl will affect Kino & his family?
6. What do you think is going on in Juana's mind?

<u>Connections</u>: What did today's reading remind you of?

It reminded me of Black Boy because both the mother in Black Boy and the baby in The Pearl were refused medical help because of their race.

FIGURE 7–2. Discussion starter sheet

HINTS FOR SUCCESSFUL LITERATURE CIRCLES

1. Create literature circles where each successive opportunity gives students a broader scope and increasing accountability, perhaps like this:

- Practice/demonstration: Each group practices with the same short, simple work.

Passage Finder

Name __Chris R._____ Group __2__

Book ___The Pearl_____

Meeting Date __3/5/_____

Assignment: Pages __21__ to __40__

Passage Finder: Your job is to locate paragraphs from the reading that you would like for

your group to read aloud and consider-- passages that you find interesting, important,

striking, confusing, or illuminating. Choose three passages, and decide who should read

the passages aloud, and plan how they should be discussed and examined.

Passage Finder: Your job is to locate paragraphs from the reading that you would like for

First Passage

Page # ___21___ Paragraph # ___1____

Second Passage

Page # ___26___ Paragraph # ___2____

Third Passage:

Page # ___29___ Paragraph # ___2____

Plans for reading and discussing passages:

__a volunteer will read each passage and then__

__everyone will discuss it. Each person should express__
__an opinion.__

Connections: What did today's reading remind you of?

__It reminded me of winning the lottery because when Kino__

__found the great pearl, it was as if he had won the lottery.__
Winning the lottery brings the winner jumbled emotions,
and Kino is experiencing these feelings after he
finds the pearl.

FIGURE 7–3. Passage finder sheet

- Whole class, common book: Each group reads and examines the
  same required work. (We recommend short novels like John
  Steinbeck's *The Pearl*, George Orwell's *Animal Farm*, or Sandra
  Cisneros' *The House on Mango Street*.)

- Six groups read six different works, categorized by genre and/or theme.
- Students choose genre, books, groups.

2. Keep a 5″ × 8″ index card—just one for each class will do—to chart students' progress. For each literature circle session, give students two grades, one over the other, like this: A/B+. The first grade indicates completion of the role sheets (in most cases, this amounts to either A or F—it's either done or it's not—and the teacher and group members need to counsel those who are not fulfilling their roles). The second grade is a process grade that the teacher assigns to each student based on her own observations of that student interacting with the group and any assessment questions students have written. The teacher can then use these grades, in addition to any final evaluation rubrics or activities.

3. Integrate literature circles into standard curriculum in the same way you would integrate reading/writing workshops. For example: Monday and Thursday, the teacher plans literature circles. On Tuesday and Wednesday, she gives whole-class instruction, perhaps notes, lecture, and discussion. On Friday, the teacher conducts a whole-class discussion where she calls upon each literature circle to share something with the larger group.

4. Consider having a topic or two written on the board for cases when discussions end prematurely or fall flat; this keeps the teacher from repeating a suggested discussion topic group after group, and it gives students a safety net of sorts without controlling the content or direction of their discussion too much.

5. For the beginning or closing of a literature circles class, ask students questions requiring them to assess their experiences. You might like to develop a self-assessment rubric for a particular aspect of participation, such as "My Contribution to Group Discussion." Instead of using a rubric, we periodically asked two or three questions and had students write responses on 5″ × 8″ index cards. Note these examples:
- How would you describe (or rate) your own participation in today's discussion?
- What did your group do well today? What did the group do poorly? How might you change whatever you did poorly?
- List both strengths and weaknesses in the literary circles process.
- So far, how does the literature circles experience compare to other ways of reading and studying literature?

6. To conclude the literature circles experience, ask several questions for final assessment. If most of your previous questions for assessment focused on group responsibilities and process, ask final questions that focus on both content and process; ask both simple questions (like the first one below) and challenging ones (like the second):

- Name one significant event from the book, and explain why it is significant.
- To what extent does illusion affect Kino and Juana's lives? To what extent does it affect our real lives?
- What do you see as a moral or message of *The Pearl?*
- How have your impressions about literary circles—or about the book itself—changed during the course of reading?
- Give yourself and each group member a letter grade based on how well each person carried out his roles during the course of literature circles. Give your group a letter grade based on how well it functioned. Explain your grades in writing.
- Under what circumstances would you want to participate in a literature circle again?
- What changes would you recommend for improving literature circles?

Our experiences with literature circles were positive ones where heterogeneous groups of students took on academic pursuits in a more organized and cooperative way than we had seen from other reading configurations. Using literature circles makes the sharing that occurs naturally for many students in reading/writing workshops occur deliberately for all students.

Elements of an (Impromptu) Interdisciplinary Unit Plan

Teachers are busy people, often isolated with little common preparation time. Even middle school teachers with a common prep period for team planning need quick ways to put together interdisciplinary units. At conferences and workshops, we often come across excellent but exhaustive unit plans—ones that we can't imagine writing or carrying out. We prefer creating units that are simple in setup, but not in concept or in possibilities, with the following elements:

- Introduction (brainstorming and free writing)
- Readings (response and analysis)
- An interactive activity or two

- Gathering and searching for information to inform the activity
- Assessment (writing to learn)

A teacher who wants to develop an interdisciplinary study, either by working directly with or alongside teachers and classes of another subject, can use the preceding scheme to organize a unit plan—like the one we put together on America's parks one year, when our school theme was "This Land is Your Land." Here's what we did, using the elements above and taking relatively little time.

America's Parks

Grade: 7–8
Time: five to eight class periods
Outcome: Students use the theme to brainstorm, write, read, research, and design a postcard.

Introduction. We drew up an announcement of our intended topic of study, America's parks—national parks, theme parks, ballparks, and historical landmarks—on a sheet of easel paper for use in an introductory mini-lesson. We briefly introduced the concepts of development, conservation, and preservation as they apply to our parks. Finally, we included a preliminary homework assignment for students to bring to school brochures, postcards, books, videos, maps, and manuals from any such places they have visited.

Brainstorming. For each class, we taped a large piece of mural paper to the chalkboard, put a box of markers and crayons on a nearby table, and asked students to take a marker, step up to the paper, and brainstorm. We asked students to write down any words and phrases; names and places; topics, feelings, and ideas; or symbols and icons about the theme that occurred to them. (As with all brainstorming activities, the purpose is to accept all ideas without judging or censoring them. Students should write whatever comes to mind.)

Free writing. The next day, we asked students to write freely for twelve minutes, choosing one or more of these topics: national parks, theme parks, ballparks, nature, and utopia. We asked for five volunteers to share what they wrote with the class.

Tip for success. With each successive step or activity in the interdisciplinary plan, we give students opportunities to broaden their concept of the topic or think more analytically than they may have previously done; for example, in this free writing activity, we brought the concepts of *nature* and *utopia* into the mix. For the next segment of the plan—reading, response, and analysis—we chose a piece that embodied both nature and utopia.

Reading and response. We chose two pieces for the class to read: a play about John Muir, which students read aloud in groups of four, each taking parts, and an excerpt from Emerson's "Nature." (The activity we used for reading and responding to "Nature" can be found in Chapter 1.)

Activity. Again, we chose an activity for this unit that is simple in concept and can be executed on many ability levels: Design a postcard. Each student chose one of America's parks and created both fronts and backs of the postcards, designing lettering, illustrations, and graphics for the front; and writing a three-paragraph letter on the back, including facts, at least one problem and resolution, and an opinion about the park. Students completed their postcards on two sheets of 9″ × 12″ drawing paper—one for the front, and one for the back. This enabled us to display both front and back of each postcard.

Searching for information. Students began their searches with the information they had personally gathered and brought to class. We brought a cart of books from the library into our classroom, and students went to the library and computer lab in groups to conduct research using the Internet and encyclopedias on CD-ROMs. (This is the kind of assignment where almost all sources of information are welcome.)

Assessment. For this unit, we kept our assessment simple: Students shared their postcards with the class, focusing on one problem, one possible solution to that problem, and their overall opinion of the park they researched. We graded (check, check-plus, or check-minus), then displayed student work. The unit enabled students to learn about geography, geology, crowd control, conservation, wildlife preservation, and many other topics related to our country.

Following is a sample interdisciplinary unit that will be particularly useful for seventh- and eighth-grade classes in science, social studies, and English. Teachers of those classes might successfully use the unit as written. Teachers of other levels and disciplines can apply the unit's concepts to their own lessons and units. For example, integrating a children's book or selections of poetry with social studies and science content lessons is an effective method.

A Sample Interdisciplinary Unit: Whose River Is This?

Grade: 7–8
Time: Seven to ten class periods

Outcome: After completing reading, writing, and activities, students create a mural depicting a river's cycle of growth from pristine state to ecological balance.

We developed this unit on environmental awareness to fit both our school theme for the year and our state social studies curriculum, and we presented it just as students were studying the industrial revolution. It is based on the work of teacher Anne Marie Antener of Wantagh, New York, who first showed us the activity as delivered to third graders.

In watching students engage in the required tasks, we witnessed the most striking feature of the unit: students were visibly disturbed and moved by activities that enabled them to feel the effects of creation, pollution, and regeneration. The unit includes an introduction (brainstorming and free writing), reading and discussing three poems, and completing several activities (including written assessments).

Introduction. We briefly introduced the theme of our unit: the river, especially as it connects to environmentalism and environmental history. We told students that they'd be reading, writing, and engaging in several cooperative activities, but we did not give them any leads that would spoil the effects of those activities. We had students write freely, this time in list form. We asked them to list anything that came to mind when they think of rivers. Students then scribbled words, connections, symbols, and such onto a piece of mural paper, providing a visual of their collective associations.

Reading and response. In whole-class lessons, we read aloud and discussed three poems that we had chosen to broaden students' perceptions of what rivers are and what they represent. We read each poem aloud to students two times, and then we discussed each by using the following questions. In doing so, we examined the use and importance of imagery, simile and metaphor, symbols, and allusions in poetry.

"THE FISHER" BY LYLE GLAZIER

1. Major appeal of the poem: Is it chiefly to the intellect? Emotions? Senses? What combination?
2. Do you like the poem? Why?

"THE NEGRO SPEAKS OF RIVERS" BY LANGSTON HUGHES:

1. Major simile or metaphor: Is there one governing the poem?
2. Allusions: What are they, and what do they accomplish?
3. Discuss what the river symbolizes in the poem.

1. The author alludes to many different times, places, and waterways in his poem. Name the allusions you recognize. How/why do you recognize them?
2. What do you suppose the author's intent was in writing this poem?
3. How does the length of the poem relate to the author's intent?

Creating (and Polluting) a River

Students sat in groups of four for this activity, which we took three class sessions to complete. We did not tell them, "Today we're going to create and pollute a river," or anything like that, which would ruin the effect of the activity.

Days 1 and 2. We introduced Lynne Cherry's picture book *A River Ran Wild* (1992), noting especially the historical and environmental timeline on the inside front and back covers; we had students take turns reading these timeline entries and the author's note aloud. We then began reading the story aloud to students, taking time to show illustrations; but we did not read the book all the way through. Instead, we read just the first three pages, stopping with the words, "The river, land, and forest provided all they needed." In order to set up the first segment of our activity, we wanted to stop the reading while the river in Cherry's book was still in a pristine state. We closed the book, gave each group a piece of 18″ × 24″ drawing paper, and we asked them to create (draw) and name their own river, using markers, pastels, and crayons. We encouraged students to personalize their rivers.

Students engaged immediately in their creations, and could have drawn forever, but we asked them to finish their rivers by the end of the second class. We collected the rivers.

Day 3. We finished reading *A River Ran Wild* to the students, seeing the story's Nashua River become polluted and rehabilitated. We then closed the book and shuffled and redistributed the rivers so that no group had its own river at their table. We gave students very simple instructions: "Now, pollute your river."

Witnessing and feeling students' responses shocked us. Most groups sat stunned for a few seconds before they swooped down on their rivers with fists full of black and brown markers, scribbling filth with reckless abandon. They did more than just draw objects like tires in the water and bottles on the riverbanks; they obliterated beautiful rivers a dozen black markers at a time, painting whiteout graffiti over that. What amazed all of us, we discovered, is this: creation takes time, thought, and energy, but destruction does not. It occurs in fast-accumulating split seconds, and it takes no thought.

Assessment (writing to learn). Still on Day 3 of the activity, we asked students to write about both creating and polluting a river. Their responses mirrored what we saw in their faces and bodies as they destroyed each other's rivers. Here's the question we asked, followed by student responses:

Write freely and honestly for twelve minutes: You created a beautiful river that others polluted. You polluted a beautiful river that others created. How do you feel about this creation–pollution process?

KENNY: "I liked creating a river. I thought it was a fun project that we put a lot of work into. It really annoyed me when a group of girls got our projects and instead of just putting some cans and other junk in the water, they didn't care about anything and just wrote all over our project and ruined all the time and effort we put into it. After all that, I scribbled all over someone else's project because I was angry. I bet a lot of other groups did the same thing."

SHANNON: "At the time, polluting a river seemed fun, but when we were finished, it was just a sloppy mess, and the people who had created it were mad. When our creation was brought back to us, you would never guess that it was once a beautiful, shining river. We were upset that all our hard work and time was destroyed in minutes."

DAVID: "I enjoyed drawing our river. It took hard work and effort, and to see it destroyed was almost heartbreaking. It made me very angry. It also angered my group, who was busy taking out their anger on another defenseless river. I learned how fragile nature is and how easily it can be affected by pollution."

TIM: "This project does tie in well with real life. The most careful creators get a good river, and the most careless and deliberate polluters get an unsalvageable river. I wish somehow, though, that more people would get it through their heads that this is happening in real life and go do something about it. Maybe then we'd help fix one of the earth's problems."

Culminating activity. Creating a mural as a culminating activity, we did two things: first, we gave groups the opportunity to recreate or redesign their original rivers, in which many had taken a personal interest. Our second and ultimate project was to create a mural depicting a river's movement and growth through the following states:

- Pristine state
- Settlement
- Industrialization
- The river in jeopardy

- Cleanup
- Ecological balance

We divided the mural into six panels, one for each state of the river's development, and we taped each panel to a chalkboard or wall, setting up six stations around the room. We gave students lessons on how to create panels that reflected individual choices, but that also flowed artistically from one to the other. Watercolors and pastels, markers and crayons, colored chalk and charcoal—we used these media to create "Rolling River." When the river mural was finished, we displayed it along with students' polluted rivers and responses.

Final Assessment. Once we had finished and displayed our mural, we asked students to write freely, responding to the following prompts. We then shared and posted a variety of these responses.

Regarding our river project:

- What did you feel about the project? What did you learn from it?
- How is creating a mural different from individual and small group tasks?
- Suggest specific ways in which river themes could be studied in your math and science classes.

Note these two representative responses:

KRISTIN: "I learned a lot from the river project. Nature is a delicate balance: so easy to destroy, so difficult to regenerate. I believe that was the essence of this project. Creating a mural really brought me closer to my classmates. Group cooperation and awareness of activity around us was key. Compromise and improvisation were all around, which I preferred to the usual arguments. While creating the mural, we didn't care whether we liked each other or not; somehow we found a balance. I hope someday we can find a balance with nature as well."

TERRY: "I enjoyed working on this project; I felt that it really taught the value of a clear and healthy river, and how in a short time it could be destroyed. Creating the mural was different from our other tasks because it combined art and thought together. The mural was the best part of this project. Creating a mural gave you a visual of the river's cycle. One specific way we could use the river theme in math could be, maybe finding and comparing the rate at which different rivers flow. Another idea we could try is to find how much water a river contains in cubic centimeters. For science, we could look at the high and low points and try to determine when they will occur again. We could also look at the chemical readings in various rivers and determine which rivers are least polluted, which are most heavily polluted."

Alternative Activity: Titles Exercise

Grade: 7–12
Time: One class period
Outcome: In creating titles for a piece of their choice, students closely examine their own writing.

This activity works well in a heterogeneous class. It provides a method that enables each student to think about a piece of writing in divergent ways. Students need a pen, a blank sheet of paper or two, and a significant draft of their writing (or a piece of free writing that they think has potential) in order to complete this exercise.

So that students reap the benefit of rethinking or recasting their own writing, it is best if the teacher conducts a whole-class exercise, reading each of the twenty topics aloud to the class, repeating each topic once (giving further explanation sparingly) and giving students a minute or so to come up with a title for each.

Not providing students a copy of the exercise enables the teacher to present an effective lesson in listening skills that will work in heterogeneous groupings: students can't compete by looking ahead or moving faster. They have to consider their writing in light of each given prompt.

Teachers can shorten this exercise, of course—it's a more arduous task than it first appears to be—but a good deal of its worth is in its intensity. Students' listening skills, thinking skills, and writing will benefit by doing all twenty.

TITLES EXERCISE
1. Copy a sentence from your draft that could serve as a title.
2. Write a sentence that is not in your draft that could serve as a title.
3. Interrogative title: write a title in the form of a question.
4. Write a title beginning with the word "in."
5. Pick out a concrete image—something the reader can hear, see, smell, taste, or feel—to use as a title.
6. Choose a color that represents your piece of writing.
7. Create a title that contains a hot or cold image.
8. Create a title comparing your writing to an animal.

9. Write a title that begins with an "ing" word.
10. Use a word ending with "est" somewhere in your title.
11. Create a title that is a lie about your piece.
12. Create a very obvious one-word title for your writing.
13. Create a less obvious one-word title.
14. Write a three-word title.
15. Create a title with the name of a school in it.
16. Think of a movie, TV show, or song title that might also serve as a title for your piece.
17. Think of a particular place that represents your writing, and use that as your title.
18. Think of a person you know or a famous person whose name could serve as your title.
19. Choose an object that represents your piece of writing.
20. Look over the titles you have written so far, and pick two that might fit together. Join these two together with a colon.

Use this exercise as students are revising drafts of their writing, when they are almost ready to prepare final papers.

8

A Class Act
Demonstrations and Simulations for Learning

"A little knowledge that acts is worth infinitely more than much knowledge that is idle."
—Kahlil Gibran

If we listen to students, it's clear that what creates disinterest in classrooms is a presentation or long lecture that disconnects or separates learners from the subject matter. The simple truth is this: students don't learn if they aren't drawn to participate. Effective teachers have long understood that being drawn in is the key for students to learn and retain new material. How can we design activities with this objective? We must lead reluctant students to participate. How can teachers foster the feeling that joining in will be better than sitting passively or acting in counterproductive ways? Perceptive teachers know that to interest disinterested students they must design lessons that do the following:

- Devise situations that have a personal appeal.
- Make what happens in the classroom important and practical.
- Challenge students to interact and get involved.

We must create events in the classroom that *depend* on students getting involved in short and varied interactive demonstrations or simulations that require students to act as active participants.

Setting the Stage: Teaching by Demonstration and Simulation

Teaching by simulation differs fundamentally from the full-blown projects that many teachers may have become accustomed to. We may remember the celebration of Dickens' England, for which half of the library was transformed to resemble a street in London during the 1850s, or projects like these. These required intense work and coordinated efforts to be successful. Certainly students can benefit by participating in these activities and enhance their understanding of course material. But these projects can be time-consuming for students and teachers, and may be so overwhelming in scope that all involved become exhausted by the mere thought.

Teaching by simulation is more like the ease we might experience in starting a pickup softball game in the park rather than planning an entire formal tournament. It is a method that can easily be integrated into a lesson at any point in its development. A simulation prepares and assists students to see significant points or to help students understand or reflect on what they have learned. The simulations can be set up quickly and require little in the way of materials to gather or distribute. Here's a simulation we've used as part of a test:

In preparation for a final test on John Knowles' novel *A Separate Peace*, we clear a table in the front of the room and place several items on it. We proceed with this introduction:

> Recently, several confusing and mysterious items were discovered in a locked closet at the Devon School. Because of your expertise, you've been called in to investigate this find and offer some definitive explanations and connections. Take a look at these five items: a ski pole, a broken tree limb, a World War II recruitment poster, a pink shirt, and a gavel. Explain in writing the meaning of *three* of these items. Discuss how the item specifically relates to a significant issue, character, or event in the novel.

Tip for success. The items used in this simulation (a ski pole, a broken tree limb, a World War II recruitment poster, a pink shirt, and a gavel) will prompt students to respond to key events or concepts presented in the novel. For example, students might explain that the ski pole relates directly to the misguided enlistment and disillusionment of one of the naive boys at the Devon School who fantasized that he would contribute to the war effort as a ski trooper in the Alps. This character soon learns, after enlisting, that the war is real and the training more harsh than the recruiter had revealed. His cross-country ski regimen at Devon in no way prepared him for the reality of war. And in like manner, each item can prompt students to respond with insight and comprehension—and perhaps with slightly different interpretations.

This simulation—asking students to act as experts and make associations using these physical items—encourages students to make meaning of a text beyond the ways that some traditional comprehension activities might. The simulation invokes an atmosphere in which critical thinking and synthesis of the text occur. This method lets students demonstrate their understanding of the text and discover relevant conclusions. The physical prompts draw students in because it is a bit unusual to work this way in a classroom.

Students are intrigued with this simulation, especially if they are successful and get credit for their responses. It's uncommon to ask them to show their understanding in this way. With imagination and a collection of items, pictures, or audio aids (or any prompts you can gather), teachers can adapt this simulation to any piece of literature or unit of study. Practice this technique as a class activity or use it as a quiz so that students gain some familiarity with this method.

Simulating Real-Life Experiences

Biggs' Beans, Inc.

Why should we simulate a situation that our students will encounter in literature? Primarily because a simulation has valuable impact and resounding results to help students make meaning. While simulations may take on different looks, they are aimed at the same target: getting students to see themselves as active participants in their learning. This hands-on approach works well for many students and serves to enrich others accustomed to a steady diet of traditional learning methods.

"The Trouble in Biggsville," one simulated scenario we've used, replicates conditions during an economic depression so that students can appreciate the plight of the migrant workers in Steinbeck's *Of Mice and Men*. Students assume various roles in this simulation: owners of the Biggs' Beans, Inc., workers in the factory, stockholders, and bankers. There is no script to memorize or skit to perform, only a suggestion that students respond in their roles as they think appropriate. The simulation goes like this:

"Melissa, Rachel, Justin, and Jamie, you are members of the Biggs family. You own a *once*-profitable baked beans factory in Biggsville. The company has been in your family for generations, and it keeps the town running because it employs many of the townspeople. I want you to respond to some questions about your company. Carla, Don, Colin, and Ray, you're factory workers at the Biggs' Beans factory. Carla, you've worked there for thirty years, and you've just been laid off. I need each of you to respond to some questions about your jobs and your feelings about what happened to Carla. Robert, Amanda, and Tara, you're all major stockholders in Biggs' Beans, Inc., and you've got some complaints about high salaries and low profits. I'd like you to share those concerns in a few minutes. Okay, who's left? Cara, Lisa, and Brian, you're the *big* bankers in Biggsville. You've been lending money to the townspeople, left and right, because they've been buying cars and homes, putting in pools, and so on.

You're upset because some people aren't paying their loans. And finally, John, Martha, James, and Melanie, you live in Valleyside Heights, and you've recently started your own baked beans factory with modern equipment, a good product, and a high-powered advertising campaign. You're selling lots of beans cheaper than Biggs' Beans. Get ready to explain why you are successful and wait until I ask you to respond to some questions about your business. . . ."

The improvisational dialogue begins to evolve. We ask students to respond and play these parts. And there will always be one student who asks, "Can I be a banker? I don't want to be a worker in the factory." We handle such a request quickly and make the trade, not letting this become the focus of the activity. The script is in many ways improvisational—with the teacher guiding the direction of the discussion and perhaps ending the simulation at a point that will transition nicely into a discussion of the text.

Students are not worried about remembering lines or information or prescriptions of what to do. What happens depends on the craftsmanship of the teacher. We want them to respond extemporaneously to questions and react naturally to each other. Set up scenarios like these and ask them to react impromptu—the results are amazing and easily connected to the lesson of the day. Here are some sample questions we asked in this simulation.

TO THE BIGGS' FAMILY

- What is the history of Biggs' Bean, Inc., and its importance to Biggsville?
- What economic trouble are you facing?
- What will you do?

TO THE FACTORY WORKERS

- What will you do now that you got laid off by the company?
- How do you feel about someone who has been a loyal employee for thirty years losing her job?
- What worries you about your situation?

TO THE BANKERS

- Why aren't people paying back their loans?
- What will you do with new loan applicants?
- How can you get your money back?

TO THE OWNERS OF THE "NEW" BEAN FACTORY

- Why is your company selling more beans than the Biggs' Beans company?

- How are you able to keep your workers employed?
- Do you have any suggestions for the workers in Biggsville?

Follow-up questions rely on students' responses. We orchestrate the scenario to uncover our students' knowledge, perceptions, and feelings. We end by summarizing the effects of a depression on people as revealed by students and get everyone in the class to join the discussion.

In a simulation, students *feel* the emotional and psychological impact of a suggested situation. Some will opt to participate only marginally, yet the scenario has attracted them and leads to a personal interaction with the text they will read. "The Trouble in Biggsville" simulation, or any other you choose to create and use, becomes a familiar point of reference throughout the reading of the text and class discussions. In many ways, the simulation is more real to students than the text written in the 1930s. We've achieved our purpose to engage students.

Impromptu Town Meeting

If you'd like students to discuss an issue, debate a topic, or resolve a problem, a town meeting simulation works well. It's an excellent class activity adaptable to many situations. You can easily transform this concept to resemble a specific organization, company, task force, or any particular group meeting that you might imagine. The objective is to get students talking about an issue that they have feelings about.

The town meeting can be designed quickly. You need several defined roles (a mayor, historian, etc.), a few impassioned speakers (students who will speak up), an audience of concerned citizens (the majority of the class), and a "hot issue" (maybe one related to the literature you're reading). Students discuss and reflect in a forum beyond the traditional classroom. The teacher can act as mediator, at first, and take on less responsibility as the activity unfolds and students become accustomed to the format. At the end, it's important for the teacher to recap what has occurred in the meeting.

A possible scenario begins with a short statement by the mayor, a brief report by the town historian, and necessary announcements by the town manager. (You may have to give students some suggestions if this is a prereading activity.) The mayor calls for speakers, calls for questions, and mediates the discussion. The council members listen and then vote. The town manger calls for a vote on the issue(s). The town historian records the vote by the town council.

The purpose of the meeting is to explore and resolve a concern brought to the council by speakers. The only *requirement* for the meeting is to have a controversial issue and have opposing views represented by several speakers. The meeting should move quickly, unless an extended debate occurs, and might last about fifteen or twenty minutes. The town council members vote upon a resolution at the conclusion of the meeting. It is not necessary that students know the literature from which you draw the issues. The situation is the focus. Students function remarkably well in this simulation and rely on their critical thinking and analytical skills. Here's a sample town meeting activity related to Steinbeck's novel *The Pearl*.

Grade: 9–12

Time: Part of one class session

Objective: To engage students in conversation leading to an understanding of key concepts in a piece of literature

LA QUINTA TOWN MEETING, OCTOBER 17, 1999, TOWN HALL 7:00 P.M.

Defined Roles:

Mayor   Opens the meeting, states the issue, recognizes speakers, closes the meeting

Town Historian   Recalls past events, decisions, and records current actions

Town Manager   Provides any statistical, financial, or logistical information; calls for a vote

Town Board Council   Voting members who must resolve the issue (Choose an uneven number.)

Speakers at Large   Audience speakers who can present opposing views (limit this to a few); in this case, pearl buyers, consumers, and pearl fishermen are natural choices

Materials   A table, chairs, or set of desks facing the class; one seat, podium, or desk facing the council

Paper for the historian

3″ × 5″ cards for voting council (two cards each—one *yes* and one *no*)

Write this on the board:

Issue   Loss of major revenue because local pearl fishermen refuse to sell their pearls to village buyers. They have united in an effort to sell all their pearls in La Paz, the capital city.

Purpose of the Meeting   (1) To discuss the cause of this situation; (2) to determine how to prevent this loss of revenue; (3) to vote upon immediate action to take

The Vote   The town council votes as individuals (it's best to have an uneven number). In this scenario, they vote on a proposal to stop pearl fishermen from selling their pearls in La Paz or a compromise to the situation. Connect and apply *any* decision to the novel.

Tip for success: For a follow-up activity audience members should write and share their comments about the meeting and final vote. These can be informal journal reactions or more formal letters/editorials. Encourage students to react to the proceedings and share personal perceptions. End the class with a discussion to relate the issues revealed in the meeting to *The Pearl*.

The meeting format can be easily integrated into literature study at any point (before reading a chapter or after reading a particularly meaningful scene). Adapt/change the roles to meet your needs and the issues you want to examine. Here are several we've used:

- A town meeting to discuss the jury's verdict in *To Kill a Mockingbird*
- A neighborhood meeting to discuss Eddie Carbone's betrayal in *A View from the Bridge*
- A bunkhouse meeting to discuss Lennie's transgression in *Of Mice and Men*
- A company meeting to discuss Willie Loman's dismissal in *Death of a Salesman*
- A faculty meeting to discuss Holden Caulfield's expulsion in *The Catcher in the Rye*
- A senate meeting to discuss Brutus' action against Caesar in *Julius Caesar*
- An assembly to discuss law and order on the island in *Lord of the Flies*

The meetings should have a clear objective and shouldn't disrupt the flow of a lesson. It's best to keep the meetings short and end them when students have revealed a significant point or reached some useful conclusion. Monitor this carefully and decide when to step in. Keep in mind that the intent of much of the meeting is improvisational; this is part of its fascination and appeal.

Inspirational Video Clips

How do teachers use films or videos in the classroom? Typically many teachers show entire videos, often in segments over several days. We may use a video or film to supply background for students about a particular subject like

Shakespeare's England; to bring a novel to life like Orwell's *1984*; to give a script voice like Williams' *The Glass Menagerie*; to compare interpretations of different mediums like the film and text versions of Jackson's "The Lottery." Using videos is embedded in teachers' methods. We show them; students react favorably and often learn through this medium. We'd like to suggest several *effective alternatives* using short video *clips* rather than showing entire films (you may have to show the clip several times):

1. Compare video clips of similar scenes in different versions of the same film. There are many remakes available that make this possible. Ask students to react to the different versions. It increases their ability to analyze a film and view it critically. They note a film's intention, effect, and meaning.

2. For a writing activity, show a video clip *without sound* in which characters speak and gesture. (You can find excellent scenes in almost any film, but it works best to choose ones with which students are unfamiliar.) Have students individually, in pairs, or in a group to write a possible dialogue they imagine would best fit the scene and characters. Assign the parts and share these aloud as the silent video clip plays. Discuss the decisions, and show the scene with the original soundtrack added.

3. Show a silent scene (openings, closings, or action-packed scenes work well) and have students suggest what sound effects and what type of music would be appropriate to use to add meaning. Comparing student suggestions with the original provides an interesting learning experience. Students see how sound effects and music create mood, meaning, or feeling.

4. Show a video clip (without spoken text) of a landscape, vista, or setting and let students write an accompanying text. Let the student-generated texts act as a narrator's voice-over to provide commentary that can be read while the video plays. This works well to emphasize the effect of specific word choice, appropriate sentence length, and appropriate pace.

Don't hesitate to stop a video and ask students to offer comments or suggest meaning about what they've just seen. Stop the video and ask students to predict what will happen. Prepare them to hear a speech by asking them what their expectations might be. The keys are this: stop the video, talk briefly, and continue the clip. You will see an increased attentiveness to the video.

Engaging Methods: The Button Demonstration

A lot of literature we assign, read, and discuss depicts characters who make decisions that significantly affect their lives. There are few pieces of literature in which decision making is not a relevant issue. The button demonstration (or any adaptation you devise) gives participants experience in making choices that students in the class can witness, discuss, and write about in a nonthreatening atmosphere. For example, this works well as a prereading activity for literature in which characters must face the consequences of their actions, fair or unfair. Students see that decisions have consequences: sometimes these consequences are just, other times they are not. In the button demonstration, you can manipulate the consequences to make a point. Here's how the demonstration goes:

Draw a button on the board that is large enough for the class to see. Above the button write in bold letters DO NOT PUSH. (See Figure 8–1.) Without any discussion, select several students to participate (about five or six) and have them individually go up to the board and *react in some way* to the sign and the button. No instructions and no answers to any questions are necessary. (Students read the sign and choose to push or not to push the button.) The rest of the class should record the action, reaction, and consequence of each participant. You can construct a simple action/consequence chart on the board to help.

DO NOT PUSH

FIGURE 8–1. Button sign

Have the consequences (a variety of written statements you've prepared) ready to give to each participant after a decision has been made; you choose which you'll give out based on the action of the student. Print the statements and cut them into strips so that each participant can receive a different comment. Each participant should read the statement silently first and then aloud to the class. Here are several consequences we've used for pushing or not pushing the button:

> YOU LOSE ! NICE TRY. THINK HARDER NEXT TIME. I'M FEELING GENEROUS, SO THERE'S NO PENALTY. GO QUIETLY. YOU'VE BEEN SPARED.

> CAN'T YOU READ? I CAN'T BELIEVE YOU DID THAT. WHICH WORD DON'T YOU UNDERSTAND? I HOPE YOU LEARNED SOMETHING FROM THIS LIFE EXPERIENCE. DO NOT PASS GO, DO NOT COLLECT $200—GO STRAIGHT TO JAIL.

> WAY TO GO . . . YOU HAVE JUST RELEASED A DEADLY POISON—IT'S IN THE CHALK—YOU AND THE FIVE PEOPLE CLOSEST TO YOU HAVE ONLY SECONDS TO LIVE. WHAT ARE YOUR LAST WORDS BEFORE YOU GO TO THAT BIG BUTTON FACTORY IN THE SKY?
> (P.S. BREATHE DEEPLY—YOU'RE USING OUR AIR.)

> GOOD FOR YOU—WAY TO GO! YOU ARE A PERSON WHO THINKS FREELY AND MUST BE REWARDED . . . YOUR CAREFUL DECISION HAS PAID OFF. YOU WILL RECEIVE A CHECK FOR $20 MILLION.

> ARE YOU AFRAID TO ACT UPON YOUR TRUE FEELINGS? TRY BEING HONEST FOR ONCE . . . IT WILL SERVE YOU BETTER IN LIFE. SIT DOWN QUICKLY.

> OKAY, NOW WHAT? DO YOU EXPECT TO BE REWARDED JUST FOR FOLLOWING THE RULES? WHY? YOU ACTED AS EXPECTED, SO SIT DOWN, THAT'S IT . . . THERE'S NOTHING MORE. (SOME PEOPLE ARE NEVER SATISFIED.)

> I'M SORRY YOU HAVE CHOSEN NOT TO ACT. PLEASE REPORT TO THE FEDERAL MAXIMUM SECURITY PRISON TOMORROW. YOU WILL SERVE A LIFE SENTENCE FOR YOUR DECISION.

These statements and consequences for acting or not acting can initiate the following discussion and writing topics:

- Conformity and Nonconformity
- Obedience and Disobedience
- Fairness and Unfairness
- Fortune and Misfortune
- Jealousy and Resentment

Interesting reactions occur when the consequence does not match the action—when participants who obey are punished, and those who disobey are rewarded. Ask all students to write about the results they witnessed. Class discussion reveals that students have well-defined moral beliefs, a general code of ethics, and a strict sense of fair play. Use this information in literature study to make it relevant and interesting.

A short demonstration like this can energize a classroom. Students enjoy being called upon and understand (after several of these during the course of the year) that the situation is not real (and not the primary focus) but is only being used as an example to focus on an idea that is related to the lesson.

Literature Strategy: Making Applications

Another intriguing method to prepare students to read a difficult work is creating and using a modernization. The modernization should achieve these objectives:

- Make the situation current
- Highlight major themes
- Illustrate major characters
- Clarify important relationships in the story
- Provide applicable connections

Recasting and writing a *modified* version of a piece of literature that students will read gives them a tangible connection to literature that might otherwise seem inaccessible to them. Students are better able to engage the actual text and understand the work when they have a companion text. Many students are less apprehensive about reading a major work of literature after they've experienced a preparation activity like this. Shakespeare's plays are natural candidates for this activity. Here's a *Macbeth* modernization as an example of what you might create to companion other plays or texts that students may find overwhelming.

A *Macbeth* Modernization: Max and Margie

Grade: 9–12

Time: Two class sessions

Outcome: To engage students in thoughtful discussion leading to understanding of key concepts in literature

Max and Margie, high school juniors at Birnam Woods High School, have developed a close relationship. Planning to attend college after graduation, they've both applied to Dunsinane College. After college, they plan to buy land in the country and build their dream home.

Max has built a positive reputation for himself at BWHS and has gained the respect of many faculty members and students. Max worked hard to achieve his class rank of number 2 in the school. Involved in many school activities, as a junior he was named honorable mention all-region soccer player, after he guided his team to second place in the state rankings. Proud of his accomplishments, Max thrives on the attention others show for his dedication, loyalty, and hard work. Having received honors for his scholastic and athletic endeavors, Max craves more popularity and wants to be the best.

Max's closest friend, Bert, is someone with whom Max can discuss personal matters. Bert knows that Max often feels insecure about his capabilities and future, although Max hides this feeling. Max generally acts confident and poised. It's clear that Max sometimes envies Bert, who is less ambitious and not driven to succeed, yet is intelligent and an all-state wrestler.

One person in the school, Donald, exceeds Max's reach both academically and athletically. Donald, senior class president and valedictorian, has received a full academic scholarship to prestigious Inverness University. Donald, also popular in school, treats everyone equally and with respect and is not boastful of his achievements. Donald likes Max and has helped him become a successful student and athlete. He has included Max in school activities so that everyone could see what outstanding attributes Max possesses. He plans to help Max obtain a scholarship to I.U. next year. Donald has often acclaimed Max as a model student and expects that Max will be elected class president. Concerned about BWHS, Donald wants to leave the school in good hands when he graduates.

Recently, Max has had disturbing dreams and felt terrible anxiety about his position in the school. The strange dreams suggest that to get his scholarship and become "number 1" at BWHS, it would be easier if Donald were not around. Max resents Donald's brotherly behavior and feels that he could accomplish his goals without his help. He does not want to exist in Donald's shadow.

These unsettling feelings upset Max, so he confides in Margie. Her reaction shocks Max. Not only does she understand his situation, but she also scolds him for being so timid to have let this situation go on for so long. She encourages Max to take aggressive action. Together they discuss a plan to destroy Donald's popularity and reputation in the school. They plan to invite Donald to a party and initiate his undoing. Using a chemical that induces alcoholic intoxication, Max and Margie plan to put Donald in a compromising position. Max will slip the potent chemical in Donald's soft drink just before he leaves the party. Margie will call the police and register a complaint about a drunk driver that she encountered on the road. She will give a full description of the car, the license plate, and the driver. If timed properly, Donald will be stopped and arrested for driving while under the influence of alcohol. Max has some misgivings, but Margie goads him to carry out the plan.

On the night of the party, Max is nervous and suggests they abandon their scheme. Once again, Margie lectures him and convinces him to follow through with their original intentions. The first part of plan works as designed, except for one flaw. The police, having to respond to another call before investigating Margie's complaint, do not intercept Donald leaving the party. Severely affected by the powerful chemical, Donald loses control of his car at high speed on the expressway. He hits a light pole and is killed!

News of this accident stuns the community and school. Max and Margie learn of the accident the next morning when a local news broadcast shows footage of the demolished car and police removing a body from the wreckage. Max goes into shock, consumed by his own guilt. He calls Margie to discuss this situation and determine how they should react to it.

Here are several discussion or writing suggestions to use with *Max and Margie:*

- Discuss what motivates Max to act. Discuss the consequences of Max and Margie's actions.
- Identify two reasonable alternatives for Max to reach his goals.
- Discuss Margie's responsibility in this incident. To what extent is she to blame?
- List options for Max and Margie after the news of the accident is released.
- Discuss feelings that Max and Margie *might* have after Donald's death.

To culminate this discussion or writing activity, it's important to link this modernization to the actual play. Clearly illustrate how these characters relate to Macbeth, Lady Macbeth, Banquo, and Duncan in *The Tragedy of Macbeth*. In discussing any modernization or modified story, it's necessary to highlight a variety of relevant connections. Students recognize more easily the important themes presented in literature when they see these ideas in a modern context. This promotes a close reading of the text.

Tip for success: Consider creating and using modified and modernized versions of major works of literature. Design them to provide background knowledge, a frame of reference, and an impetus to read the original version. This modernized version of *Macbeth* and ones like them appeal to students because they're familiar with the context of the action and can understand the motivations of the characters. They are anxious to give opinions about the situation and often have strong feelings about Max and Margie. As a result, Shakespeare's *Macbeth* takes on more relevance for students, initially, when they can relate it to their own experience. With this assistance, students make the transition to the play with more confidence and added enthusiasm.

Three-Stage Thinking and Writing: Moving to Higher Levels

After reading literature, we should motivate all students to think and write beyond literal levels. While we strive for this in all our lessons, we can specifically design activities aimed at taking our students through three distinct stages of thinking: literal, interpretive, and application. Three-stage thinking and writing activities enable students to analyze a text from these perspectives.

Here are two samples of three-stage thinking and writing activities, one designed for Walt Whitman's "I Hear America Singing," and the other, for use with William M. Clark's "The Supermen," that can be completed individually, in groups, or as a class.

Grade: 9–12
Time: One class session
Outcome: To encourage critical thinking about concepts presented in a piece of literature

Sample 1: Three-Stage Thinking and Writing Activity
Use the poem "I Hear America Singing" by Walt Whitman as your source to respond to these statements. Check the blanks of those statements in each level with which you agree. Briefly clarify/justify *one response in each stage* in your journal.

LEVEL I   What does the speaker in the poem *reveal*?

_____   a. Workers sing about their work.

_____   b. Singing workers do more work.

_____   c. Each worker has a separate song.

_____   d. Singing makes workers happy.

LEVEL II   What is the speaker's *point*?

_____   a. America needs laborers.

_____   b. We should be proud of the jobs we do.

_____   c. The sounds of individual workers working join to make one.

_____   d. Some jobs in America are not valued.

LEVEL III   What are the poem's *applications*?

_____   a. American workers must maintain pride in their work.

_____   b. America should recognize workers who make us strong as a nation.

_____   c. The sound of workers doing their jobs creates a positive atmosphere.

_____   d. America has a strong tradition of work.

Plan to share your written responses in class.

Sample 2: Three-Stage Thinking and Writing Activity

Use the short story "The Supermen" by William M. Clark as your source to respond to these statements. Decide whether you agree or disagree with each of the following statements. (Mark A or D.)

STAGE I   Literal Meaning

_____   1. George Summers took the law into his own hands.

_____   2. George fought against violence and "hoodlumism" in WW II.

STAGE II   Interpretive Meaning

_____   1. George's comments and body language suggest he is defensive and will not resist.

_____   2. George does not act impulsively but rather calculates each move he makes.

STAGE III   Extension or Application

_____   1. Young people often underestimate the older generation.
_____   2. George's actions can be considered heroic.

Work collaboratively to *prove or disprove* these statements *in writing.* Use the text as a source for your decisions and *document* your evidence.

Keep these objectives in mind as you design a three-stage thinking and writing activity for your students:

- Make the statements short in length and few in number.
- Offer both true and false statements in each stage.
- Allow for answer diversity with justification.
- Focus on the highest stage of thinking in discussion.

Tip for success: You can design these three-stage thinking and writing activities for use with any piece of literature. The result is that students enhance their ability to interpret and apply what they've read and learned.

Alternative Activity: This Is Who I Am

Often we ask students to write personal essays to make meaning of the world through recall or observation. We stress that personal commentary must accompany description. The following interview simulation encourages students to observe a scene unfolding and to make meaning of their observations.

Grade: 9–12
Time: One class session
Outcome: To encourage observation and inferential thinking

Ask for three student volunteers for this demonstration and have them leave the classroom for a few minutes. Explain to the class: when each student returns (one at a time), he or she will sit facing the class, and ten student questioners will ask the participant one question. It will be the same question: Who are you?

Questioners may use their voice, gestures, or facial expressions to give the question a personal spin, but they should all ask the same question. All students should note the reaction of the volunteer and record answers and any observations. After the third volunteer has undergone the questions, students should write in their journals about what they have witnessed and any meaning they can ascertain—inferential, comparative, or applicable to other situations. The volunteers should write about their experience.

Ask the volunteers to share their thoughts about the experience. Let students share what they have written and note these ideas on the board. Connect these notes to possible topics for writing or to situations students may find in reading literature.

Tip for success: Students go beyond simply recording literal observations or descriptions. They make meaning from their observations in thoughtful ways that can be used in writing an essay. The simulation uncovers many feelings and may evoke valuable questions for writing. Here are a few of these questions:

- What is our true identity? How many identities do we have?
- How do we define ourselves? What names/roles do we go by?
- How do we react under pressure? What defense mechanisms do we use?
- How do we communicate nonverbally? How does body language indicate what we may be feeling?
- How personal are we willing to be in public?
- How do we act when we are confused, embarrassed, or annoyed?

There are some personal risks in a simulation like this. The volunteers should feel secure in the classroom. It serves no purpose to embarrass students or cause them to feel overanxious. The possible results outweigh the minor discomfort that volunteers might feel. The focus should clearly be to improve observation skills and reflection techniques, and to make logical inferences based on the answers the interviewees offer. Encourage students to write about other observations with the intent to provide interesting personal insights and meaning.

9

Making the Academic Personal

Keeping the *I* in Learning

"To write it, it took three months; to conceive it—three minutes; to
collect the data in it—all my life."
—*F. Scott Fitzgerald*

W*ithin* the parameters of their own state's standards of learning—or core
curriculum, teachers ask students to do different kinds of writing. For example, all teachers in New York State are required to teach students to write for
the same four purposes: (1) for information and understanding, (2) for literary response and expression, (3) for critical analysis and evaluation, and (4)
for social interaction. Teachers usually have choices in what students do for
each standard: while one eleventh-grade English teacher might meet standards for analysis and evaluation by having students write literary critiques,
the eleventh-grade teacher next door accomplishes the same by asking students to articulate opposing perspectives concerning a given issue.

No matter what grade levels or courses they teach, English teachers most
likely ask students to write variations of these two types of writing:

- An autobiographical piece (including memoirs, sketches, and
  personal narratives)
- A term paper or research report (often with outlines or note cards
  and proper documentation)

We find that teachers often like taking students through the process of
writing autobiographies and just as often hate taking students through the
process of writing research papers. Likewise, while reading more than one
hundred students' autobiographies or first-person narratives can be fun, reading that many research papers can be torture.

We want to show teachers ways that enable students to have a personal
stake in what they write, both in autobiographical pieces, where we want to
help them find and use truthful voices, and in research papers, where their
inclination is to get out of as much of the work as they can.

Our chapter contains activities for teachers to use when they ask students
to write autobiographical pieces. As well, we present an alternative to the

traditional research reports or term papers that students write—an I-Search Paper, modifying Ken Macrorie's suggestions in *The I-Search Paper* (1988) to suit our own students and circumstances.

Early Childhood Photograph: Prewriting Activity for a First-Person Narrative

Grade: 7–12
Time: Once class period
Outcome: Students write their thoughts, recollections, and impressions based on (their choice of) early childhood photographs and given questions.

This is a simple prewriting activity. Ask students to bring to class a photograph or two of themselves as young children. Suggest that students look through photo albums or boxes of family pictures in order to find clear, interesting whole-body shots. In class, ask students to respond thoughtfully to these questions as they look at their photographs:

1. How old were you in the photograph?
2. Describe your surroundings. Where were you when this picture was taken? Who took the picture?
3. What happened just before the picture was taken? Where were you headed afterward?
4. What kind of shoes were you wearing? Recall what kind they might have been if you were wearing none.
5. Comment on whether you were a skinny kid, chubby, or just medium.
6. What kind of clothes did you have on in the photo? What color? Did you like what you were wearing? Did you choose your clothing, or did someone buy or make it for you? Who? Why?
7. Describe the expression on your face. Did your expression reflect what you were feeling when the picture was taken?
8. How is your hair styled? Who cut, combed, or styled it? Did you like it that way?
9. Is anyone else in the picture? If so, who are they, and why were they with you?
10. What smells do you associate with the time and place of the photograph?

Teachers and students should use these ten questions (or better yet, they should draw up lists of their own) as an exercise to spark recollections through specific images—visual, tactile, olfactory, etc.—not as required elements in a polished first-person narrative. Students should feel free to pursue any of the ten responses that triggers an interesting story or anecdote. The teacher can then guide the students through writing a single paragraph or a multiparagraph piece.

Writing the Memoir

Memoirs are autobiographical pieces that focus on the people and events of the author's life rather than on his own growth and experience. Often arranged as (a series of related) snapshots of memorable or vivid events, the writer reveals his stance as he reports and reflects upon these events and the characters involved.

Like the preceding one, this exercise serves for prewriting or inventory purposes. Use it as a prompt for when students write memoirs. It's a good idea for students to jot down a few words or phrases for each prompt, writing at greater length for any questions they choose.

Directions: Write freely, but be precise whenever you can as you respond to the following questions. Small details count—they can add up to something significant. As you write, touch upon your five senses: taste, touch, smell, sight, and hearing. Avoid being vague or general. Tell the truth, even if it is sometimes unpleasant.

1. First memories: These tend to be fragmented. Talk through these: The first things I remember are . . .
2. Before I was born: Consider parents, grandparents, how you came to live where you did.
3. A place: Remember a place from your childhood—a garden, a room, your grandparents' house, a basement, a vacation spot, a hideout . . .
4. A person: Describe someone you can see clearly: a relative, teacher, family friend, older child, bully . . .
5. A party or family gathering: Capture in words a birthday, anniversary, family reunion, funeral, holiday . . .
6. A season: Sense the images of any season—food, clothing, weather, smells, pastimes . . .

7. Things that frightened you: Recall people, performances, thunderstorms, monsters, war, tragedy . . .
8. Siblings, a best friend, or a cousin: Recall specific incidents involving them.
9. Pets: Tell how you got them and how they died.
10. Something you wanted very badly: Show how in the end, you got it or didn't.

Writing a First-Person Narrative

Grade: 8–10
Time: One class period
Outcome: Students write a first-person narrative (or memoir—several topics will adapt) on a given topic.

This assignment is uncharacteristically bookish, but for when the teacher needs a standardized writing task for students, it can be useful in either of two ways:

1. As a self-contained, timed writing sample: As states and school districts examine student performance in an ongoing effort to raise achievement and performance, schools test and assess students based on their ability to perform given reading and writing tasks in a timed setting—time for revision is not an option. Without going overboard, teachers need to give students opportunities where they can practice responding to a given assignment in a given time period.
2. As a first draft writing session to be followed by time (about two weeks) for revision, editing, and final copy preparation: Students benefit when the teacher takes an open stance to writing in his classroom and maintains an atmosphere where quality in writing is nurtured, expected, respected, and celebrated. When given time to develop drafts of their writing—that is, time to write first drafts, put them aside for a while, read them aloud to classmates, revise, edit, and prepare final copies—students invest time and interest in a piece, and their writing improves.

Directions: Write a first-person narrative using one of the following titles. You may modify titles to suit your needs. (Here's where the teacher should tailor directions to her intended use of the assignment: definition of first-person narrative or memoir, single- or multiparagraph development, suggestions for revision and editing, etc.)

1. The Nerve of Some People
2. The Worst Party I Ever Attended
3. My First Fight
4. We Moved to a New Neighborhood
5. The Day I Learned Fear
6. My First Experience As a Babysitter
7. A Trick That Backfired
8. My First Night Alone
9. I Fought for My Rights
10. The Day My Pet Died
11. A Frightening Experience
12. I Scored the Winning Basket
13. My Ordeal With Braces
14. I Was So Embarrassed I Wanted to Die
15. We Lost the Game
16. The Dumbest Thing I Ever Did
17. A Halloween to Remember
18. It Happened at the Beach
19. A Day I'll Never Forget
20. My First Date Was Almost My Last

Autobiography Poems

Grade: 8–12

Time: One period for the teacher to introduce the lesson and for students to begin first drafts; two or three weeks for development thereafter.

Outcome: Students write poems chronicling events, people, and places in their lives.

This activity is based on Lawrence Ferlinghetti's poem "Autobiography," essentially a series of random memories, allusions, and images that recreate the author's life. It's an efficient and engaging activity for all writers, enabling all participators to capture their lives in poetry. As an autobiographical stream of consciousness, the lesson elicits genuine student response. Here's what you do:

1. Read (excerpts from) Ferlinghetti's poem. Define and identify allusions; discuss what the allusions, specifically and in general, bring to the poem.

2. Present this definition to students: the autobiography poem is made up of a series of personal memories—mental snapshots of big and small events in your life. The memories/events may be in any order: random, chronological, thematic—you decide.

3. Show students how to write an autobiography poem. Write a series of personal memories, each as a separate line or two of the poem. Write freely. If you wish, begin each line or memory with a subject–verb combination like these:

> I saw . . .
> I knew . . .
> I dreamed of . . .
> I flew into . . .
> I screamed . . .
> I touched . . .
> I heard . . .
> I played . . .
> I lied when . . .
> I suffered at . . .
> I cried . . .
> I met . . .
> I pretended . . .
> I loved . . .

4. Once you have shown students the concept, allow them to write freely for as much time as possible. It's a good idea to provide some instrumental music as a background for students' writing—choose a mainly quiet and soothing piece, but one that has variations in tempo, intensity, and urgency. Two autobiography poems follow—the first written by a teacher executing the assignment with his classes, and the second written by a student who wishes to remain anonymous. (To accompany Ferlinghetti's title, we dropped the "ical' suffix when choosing the title "Autobiography Poems" for the lesson.)

AUTOBIOGRAPHY

I have heard the clang of 10,000 lockers
and stalked the tiled hallways past
miles and miles of kaleidoscope classrooms.

Voices drifted out,
speaking in tongues of a thousand shapers:
Copernicus, Jefferson, Dickens, Pythagorus,
Flaubert, Freud, Shakespeare, Picasso,
J. D. Salinger.
The voices take me back.
I am a boy in Flushing (funny name,
sound of toilets) where a beech tree weeps
near a Quaker house, while all around
apartment buildings sprout higher than oak trees.
I rode a Schwinn down the hills of Kissena
where fat carp dined on Wonder Bread.
I liked Ike.
I knew that Korea was overrun with red gorillas.
Jersey was summer then.
Country girls with scraped knees ran through my life.
I worried about girls,
my complexion,
wearing glasses,
being tough,
math.
I have been around the world with Bo Diddly,
On Blueberry Hill with Fats,
traded youth with Elvis.
Shaven-headed,
I have ridden Greyhounds all night
with Semper Fi still echoing through the weekends
on Holden's streets.
I went on the road with Kerouac.
I stared doom in the eye on an October day
as Jack and Niki played chicken in Fidel's yard.
I ordered lunch—hot pastrami—while Jackie screamed
in the back seat of a limo
in Dallas.
I heard the bullets keep ringing out
and smelled the stench of war wafting
through news print
and air waves
while skinny girls blew soap bubbles at
Woodstock.
I was glad to welcome a long sea wave
to the churning, pebbled shore of Montauk
where I once shared a boulder with a swashbuckling tern.
I tip-toed past Watergate, the Ayatollah,

gas lines, leisure suits, Reaganomics,
Bull markets, baby boomers, and gray hair.
But the clang of lockers
and the drone of voices
still call cadence for my march.

Richard Weissmann

WAX LIPS

It was the summer of '94 &
my brother &
I were around in my backyard
playing got ya last
as we ate wax lips.
I was nine when
My parents got divorced I was
very confused
and did not know very much
about what was going on. So I took
the art of music
up,
the art of guitar,
getting rid of my frustration
& anger.
I went to my first concert
when I was twelve, heard
Widow Maker at Jones Beach.
I was a big fan of theirs.
Now I'm fourteen &
I have a lot of things straightened
out in my life but sometimes
I still feel like I want to
be that little kid
again running around the backyard
with my brother
eating wax lips.

The I-Search Paper . . . as Opposed to the Traditional Research Paper

Note the question we use to introduce the I-Search paper: we ask students to comment upon each of the answer choices before they arrive at the correct one: (E) all the above.

Question: At its worst, what is a traditional term paper or research report?
(A) An exercise in badly done bibliography
(B) An introduction to the art of plagiarism
(C) Alien to its writer
(D) A triumph of meaninglessness
(E) All the above

Veteran teachers can tell enough stories to substantiate (E) as the best answer; new teachers can recall stories of their own experiences as students. Note these:

- Exactly Thirty Sources: The research paper is (A) an exercise in badly done bibliography when a teacher requires students to have exactly thirty sources, or any such arbitrary or outlandish edict, each listed on a note card and on a "Works Cited" page. We know teachers who do this every year; one even gave a student a failing grade for turning in twenty-nine instead of thirty note cards.
- Changing "House" to "Abode": The research paper is (B) an introduction into the art of plagiarism when students don't develop skills in text weaving (discussed in Chapter 6). Instead, they print reams of pages from their computer or line up at the copy machine. They think that copying pages from an encyclopedia and changing every seventh word—changing "house" to "abode," for example—is what writing a research paper means. They don't think of research as making and supporting an assertion or synthesizing information.
- Never Use "I" in Formal Writing: The research paper is (C) alien to its writer when the writer is warned not to use "I" in his paper. For decades, students all over America have been cautioned to maintain an objective stance when writing research papers and formal essays. Meant to teach students how to prove a point or research a topic based on proof rather than emotion, the cautionary advice often has a different effect: students detach themselves altogether and make fewer connections than they'd have made had they been taught how or when to put the "I" into their writing.
- Getting Out of Doing a Paper: The research paper is (D) a triumph of meaninglessness when the lack of voice in a paper enables a student to get out of doing it by thinly veiling someone else's term paper (plagiarizing)—or when the number of required works cited becomes the main focus. In either case, the student submits meaningless writing.
- At Its Worst: The research paper is (E) all the above.

Hyperbole aside, over the years we have discovered that allowing voice only in the form of a formal thesis or assertion hampers rather than employs students' critical research skills. We don't often expend undue energy teaching forms of academic writing. Instead, students write I-Search papers, which in the end accomplish exactly what we had always wanted to achieve through more traditional means: students engage in the processes of searching for, analyzing, writing about, and documenting information. Without being overly informal, they show voice and style in their writing.

Our primary source of information when we began using I-Search papers was a suggestion at a workshop that we read Ken Macrorie's *The I-Search Paper* (1988). We liked so much of what we read—about free writing and the I-Search paper itself—that we use the book with eighth graders, high school students, community college students, teachers, and teachers-in-training.

We explain the concept of the I-Search paper to students of all levels using these notes:

The I-Search Paper directly involves you, the writer, in both process (searching for information) and product (the writing about that search). It challenges the concept that research is the "searching again" for information already documented—for if you have never searched for information on the topic before, there is little re-search about it.

A good way to organize an I-Search paper is simply to tell the story of what you did in your search, in the order in which everything happened. Include the happenings and facts crucial to your hunt.

Macrorie suggests that if you wish, and especially for shorter papers, you can divide your paper into four parts:

1. What I knew (and didn't know) about my topic when I started out
2. Why I'm writing this paper (Here's where the writer shows how/why the search will be worthwhile/will make a difference in his/her life.)
3. The search (story of the hunt)
4. What I learned (or didn't learn). A "failed" search can be as valuable as one that succeeded.

WHAT THE I-SEARCH PAPER IS:

- Valid. By telling the story of what happened as you search for information, you enable your readers to judge the validity of your searching and finding, whereas research papers decontextualize. (Teachers can better judge the validity of students' work than they can when students use a more traditional format.)

- Useful and real. It's like the research we do in real life, where the "I" part—the narrative story of how we chose what car to buy or who we talked to about what career to pursue—is an integral part of the search.
- Designed to give you lifetime skills in listening, interviewing, reading, quoting, reporting, and writing in a way that others profit from and enjoy.
- Contemporary and interesting. It's one kind of writing that interests researchers, editors, and consumers.

Depending upon course content, I-Search paper topics can be either completely student-generated and -selected (appropriate for a writing course, for example) or thematic, where student choices relate to a given theme (appropriate for courses with interdisciplinary content—eleventh-grade English and American Studies combined, for example).

For interdisciplinary study, the possibilities are endless; teachers can adapt the I-Search to any area of study. Once teachers have chosen realms of study for their students, they need to develop assignment sheets and templates like those we've developed for the following suggested unit of study.

I-Search a Decade in Twentieth-Century America

Grade: The topic is appropriate for grades 8–11; the I-Search format is appropriate for grades 7–12

Time: Three to five weeks, interspersed with other ongoing classwork

Outcome: Students search for information and write about any one decade in twentieth century America.

You are going to search for information and write about any one decade in twentieth century America.

To make the assignment a bit broader in scope, let's add the 1890s and the 2000s to the list.

Your search for the information must include the following:

1. Choosing a topic and completing a topic organizer sheet
2. Using both traditional and multimedia resources
3. Interviewing (where appropriate)
4. Focusing on one significant, interesting person, year, or event of the decade

Early in your search, create a timeline for the decade you choose. Include varied and interesting details for each year. Complete rough notes and a final timeline, written and illustrated on 8' × 24" drawing paper.

Ultimately, you will write a fully developed I-Search paper, including the following:

1. A title page, with the title, your name, date, and teacher's name; include a picture or illustration if you choose
2. The I-Search paper itself—generally five to eight pages
3. A "Works Cited" page

This assignment's directions are simple by design—too much prescriptive categorizing would defeat the intent and spirit of the assignment. Students' searches for information take time, in class and outside of class, and they begin to jot down notes and put information together. During the weeks in which students are searching and writing (perhaps three or four, amongst other course pursuits), the teacher conducts lessons to help them formulate their papers.

Note the following suggestions for lessons throughout the I-Search process:

- Free writing: Early in their search, ask students to free write about their choices, just to get a beginning narrative voice on paper. For directed free writing, ask students to write two paragraphs:
  - What I already know about the topic and why I picked it
  - What I'd like to learn so that I'll know more about the topic
- Worksheets/Graphic Organizers: Also early in the search, it's a good idea to give students graphic organizers to help them keep track of their thoughts and findings (see Organizers A and B).

Organizer A

I-Search Topic: _____

_____

What I know about the topic: _____

_____

_____

What I need to learn so that I will know more about the topic: _____

_____

_____

Potential sources of information (human resources, companies/agencies/corporations, books, periodicals, Internet sites, etc.): _____

_____

Keep track of sources found valuable/not valuable. You'll need to know this information for your paper and for your list of sources ("Works Cited" page).

Valuable sources: _____

Not valuable sources: _____

Organizer B

Draft Due Date: _____

Working Title of Paper: _____

Your Question: _____

Personal Angle or Purpose for Writing the Piece: _____

_____

Working Thesis: _____

_____

Specific Texts, Primary Sources, and Personal Examples You Plan to Use:

_____

_____

Ideas for Opening Your Piece: _____

_____

Writing Techniques You Need to Check: _____

Comments/Questions/Suggestions: _____

_____

Hints for interviewing. Teachers might like to use these notes to conduct a lesson on interviewing. Ask students for additional hints, and have them develop appropriate questions for their own interviews.

1. Choose people who might be able to provide you with/lead you to information about your topic (decade, career, etc.).
2. Approach potential subjects tactfully. If she is willing to give you some time, schedule an interview for a mutually convenient time and place. It's your job to make your subject feel like opening up—telling a story. Feel free to let her speak; don't feel compelled to ask every question you've prepared.

3. Prepare ten or twelve open-ended questions to ask—ones for which your subject can't answer with a simple "yes" or "no." Ask follow-up questions as they pop into your head when your subject is responding to one of your prepared questions.

4. You may tape-record the interview, with your subject's permission, and/or take notes. You need not take down every word; listening is important.

5. Here are some general questions to get you started:

I-SEARCH A DECADE IN TWENTIETH-CENTURY AMERICA

- In what ways was the decade different from present day?
- What are your most striking memories from the decade?
- What one place/event/thing serves as a symbol of the decade to you?
- When you think of the decade, what person first comes to mind? Why?

Analysis and synthesis. Once students have started to come up with some information and ideas about how to present that information, we suggest using a map to help students see and feel their ways further into their topics. Figure 9–1 shows a map for use with the "I-Search a Decade" project:

Further analysis. Ask students questions like these:

1. List as many important people, facts, and occurrences as you can about the decade you've searched.
2. What conclusions can you draw about your decade based on the many facts and occurrences?
3. What themes or common denominators do you find?
4. What conflicting themes do you find?

Structuring the I-Search. Help each student discover a structure that might work best given the chosen content and direction. Discuss general possibilities with students, but let each student's content and direction drive the paper. Offer students simple methods: for a decade consumed in large part by war, like the 1940s, a basic chronological order might work: beginning, middle, end. If you present students with a more detailed, specific method of organization like the following one, make sure you allow students to deviate from it:

Paragraph 1: Why I chose the decade
2: What I already knew
3: How I went about obtaining information
4: One significant (or interesting) quality or theme of the decade
5: A more significant quality or theme

FIGURE 9–1. I-Search a decade

6: The most interesting quality or theme
7: What I learned from interviews
8: Draw conclusions—end paper with final viewpoint.

Works cited. We suggest that teachers give students as simple a structure as possible for citing the works they consult, but any structure required by English departments or school districts, such as MLA or CMS format, can work. In addition to standard formats, teachers should be sure to give students (retrieve) formats for computer software, online services, and the Internet.

I-Search evaluation. Let students know how their work will be evaluated. Teachers might like to use a rubric with college freshmen and sophomores (see Figure 9–2).

When students use the I-Search technique, they engage in real research and write vital and interesting papers. Keeping the "I" in students' research writing is an academic and personally fulfilling pursuit—a win–win outcome for teachers and students alike.

	Excellent	Good	Satisfactory	Needs Revision
Focused thesis				
MLA format throughout paper				
Well-documented				
Mechanical and technical aspects				
Citations conform to MLA standard				
Adequate supporting evidence				
Works cited				
Title				
Clarity and consistency of text				
Diction (selective word choice)				
Personal commitment in paper				
Closing				

Evaluator's Comments: _____

_____

Grade: _____

FIGURE 9–2. I-Search paper evaluation checklist

Note these excerpts from an I-Search Careers project:

DANIELLE: "I really have no idea why I decided to choose marine biology as
a career topic, other than it's the first thing that came to my
mind. A marine biologist was the first realistic thing that I could
see myself becoming, where I would be making money while

	enjoying the work. I knew that it concerned the ocean and the environment, but that's all. I wasn't sure how many years of college I would need or what I should major in. All I knew was that it had to do with a specialized area of science. I wanted to find out exactly what it involved, how much money could be earned, what colleges I should look at, how many years of college would be necessary, and the job outlook in that area."
KRIS:	"What I do with the rest of my life is a direct reflection on me and my ability to succeed. There have always been high expectations for me, from my family, teachers, and most of all myself. I want to be respected for what I do and who I am, and I don't want to let anyone down by not doing well in life. This is something that I've kept in mind throughout my search. Now that's a lot of pressure."
VINNIE:	"When I first started searching psychology, I thought I knew a lot. As I went on, I found out I didn't even understand the word itself."
ALEX:	"Like I said in the beginning, this "I-Search" is sort of a conspiracy. It's a report, something bad disguised as something good, much like the Trojan Horse."

Alternative Activity: Writing a Précis

Grade: 8–12
Time: Two or three weeks
Outcome: Students write a one-page précis based on their search for information on a topic.

When lack of time, resources, or other circumstances make it impossible for the teacher to help students through the process of writing a full-length paper, have students write a one-page précis on their topic. Writing a précis will give students practice in the kinds of skills standardized tests assess, such as the ability to summarize or draw conclusions. Students can engage in elements of the I-Search (by using Organizer A or B from this chapter, for example) without writing the I-Search paper as their culminating project. In addition, students can conduct and write interviews as separate pieces.

An Alternative for the "I-Search" Paper

Write a One-Page Précis about the Decade of Your Choice

A précis is a concise summary of the essential facts/occurrences/elements of the decade. In your précis, draw conclusions about the decade as a whole based on the details you found in your search.

Be sure that your précis accomplishes the following:

1. It relates the essence of the decade.
2. It minimizes details and examples (your timeline already addresses these).
3. It uses clear and concise language.

10
Portfolios and Other Assessments
"Did I Do This Right?"

"I through the course of this year found out that writing is an art."
—*Student comment*

H*ow* often has this happened to you? You've finished a stimulating mini-lesson preparing students to write a new piece that they'll begin in class; they appear ready—full of ideas and energy. You've given whatever directions you felt necessary, and so you turn your attention to some work you have at your desk. The room is quiet, students are working—writing. They're using the time to start a piece. Before long, several students raise their hands motioning for assistance or a few appear at your desk seeking assurance—asking something like "Am I doing this right?" or "Is this good?"

We know why many students need affirmation in the early stages of writing: they lack confidence. How can we instill self-confidence or self-assurance in our students? Well, it's not something we can provide for them in a handout or in a set of directions to follow; in fact, the more prescriptive our demands (delineated to the nth degree) the more students follow and rely on a formula, using this as the focus of what they're supposed to do. The best way to instill confidence in writers is to create an atmosphere in which the threat of failure is minimized and control over personal writing is maximized. Let the work and the decisions guiding that work take the forefront. Are there dangers inherent in this approach? Yes. Students may flounder a bit and feel uncomfortable without a rigid structure provided for them. Perhaps they might write something that is not good. Work through these stumbling blocks because the long-term benefits far outweigh this initial rough going. Encourage student writers by giving them the opportunity to do the following:

- Learn to work through these beginning obstacles.
- Gain self-confidence through trial and error.
- Learn that the initial effort does not have to be perfect.
- Learn not to settle on a first writing as a final product.
- Become more concerned about self-satisfaction.

If we don't transfer the ability to control writing to our students, they don't become writers, they merely act as writers. That's a significant distinction. A classroom is the perfect arena to let students become writers and make decisions that define them as such.

Of course this sounds reasonable in theory, but students have learned that no matter what teachers say that when they submit writing to us, we quickly become the critics, and in many cases, unforgiving judges. We've got to assure students in practice more than in rhetoric that this will not occur to a stifling degree as a piece of writing evolves. We need to consider how we evaluate student writing and the feedback we provide. This will be time well spent.

How and When We Should Assess Writing

How should we assess student writing? Provide substantive feedback throughout the process. When is it appropriate to offer suggestions or criticism? Teachers should intervene at crucial intervals. These are obvious answers to most teachers, but our actions determine how our students feel about their writing and the eventual progress they'll make. One fact is clear: we cannot let the assessment of student writing be exclusively a top-down process. If this occurs all the time, we only perpetuate the idea of a single audience. If we ask for self-assessment but do not value it or use it in any significant way, we clearly send the message to students that they are not an important part of the evaluation process. It's imperative that students continually self-assess their writing during stages in production and revision—then let others review their writing at some point. They must write about their own writing, first.

Here are two sample self-assessments (written several days apart) by a student who considers his thinking, his writing process, and the decisions affecting his writing.

JEFF'S NOTE 1

Mr. A.,

Hi! Here are all the final drafts of my stuff, not including "The Rewarding Path." I added two extra short pieces that I wrote yesterday. One is entitled "Our Government," the other is tagged "Individualism." If you have a chance to look at them and provide me with feedback, I would, as always, appreciate your guidance. "Individualism" is not as focused as I'd like it to be (bad, bad, bad). Also, you may notice that three independent clauses are linked with two coordinating conjunctions, in spite of grammatical law (I never heard of these before you told us). Also, passive voice is used to suppress the idea, which opposes my point. Passive voice is to be avoided! (Are you sure?) I believe these variations add meaning to this piece.

I wrote the other piece, "Our Government," in response to an article that appeared in the newspaper a few weeks ago concerning the town council's decision to build an industrial processing plant. I don't even live in Portsmouth, but I am seriously considering sending this to the editor of the newspaper, just to see if he (or she?) has enough guts to publish it.

Concerning my journal entry, which you kept: I committed some errors. First of all, I misspelled Pyrrho; this is a minor sin. The correct character is Pyrrho of Elis, a philosopher, c. 360–270 B.C. Secondly, (don't kill me!) after checking my source, I believe I may have misquoted him; this is a major sin. Nevertheless, I assure you that I am seeking all of the correct, relevant information I can find on Pyrrho. I am positive I can find a quote that will suit the same argument, even if it is slightly different than the one I butchered, and when I do, I'll provide you with it.

I did as you suggested and backed up my papers on my hard drive to a disk. I probably should add that I almost didn't because, after all, what is life without risk? Oh, and another thing, Bill Waverly and his hardware store have been on my mind since last Wednesday . . . maybe there is some meaning underlying my experience there. This way of writing about what we observe and experience is new to me.

I'll catch up with you,
Jeff

P.S. Don't waste your time marking this letter; I have no intention of revising it!
P.P.S. I threw another piece in at the last minute. I called it "Life."

JEFF'S NOTE 2

Mr. A.,

About the piece "Individualism." There is something that deeply concerns me about this paper. I will attempt to convey the source of this concern.

This piece occurred to me in its whole form, all at once, and without warning. As you well know, I often spend quiet time alone. Call it what you will: meditation, soul searching, self-reflection, etc. I don't think any of those labels really fit; I simply refer to it as time where I attempt to clear my mind of all thought for a while, and it brings me peace. I have done this in many places and at times which others may deem odd. It is during these times that the thought for this piece, and others like them, came to me.

What bothers me is this: I wonder if somehow I have had these thoughts for a while, but they have been subdued in my subconscious. I remember as a kid that I used to love to draw . . . well, really color. When I went to school, my teachers hindered my development by forcing me to color within the lines. In kindergarten, it is O.K. to color outside of the lines. By the time children reach second or third grade, however, we learn that the only pictures which receive praise are the ones which remain inside the boundaries: this is society. I wonder if somehow these thoughts remained in my subconscious, working themselves out, and then once they worked themselves out to the point that they meshed together correctly, they occurred to me as one concise statement.

I wonder if, in my moments of searching for meaning, these thoughts were bestowed upon me from a source of higher truth. I wonder if these thoughts, occurring suddenly and in whole form, were a revelation. I asked you before to consider several facts: (1) that this paper does not always follow correct grammatical form, (2) it contains passive voice, which teachers tell us not to use, and (3) to consider how these facts add to the meaning of the piece.

This paper and the others like it torment me. I cannot figure out where the ideas came from. It is only recently that I began to feel the necessity to trap thoughts of this type on paper. I have had these thoughts occur to me before, and I have not written them down; therefore, I forgot them. In any case, I see a certain truth in them; it is for this reason that I must save them now.

I didn't write this letter to get advice; I just felt that I should tell you, in the interest of remaining honest about my writing.

Jeff

Teachers need to provide time in class or as a homework assignment for this necessary writing to occur. Jeff's letters communicate ideas and feelings that are valuable if we are to offer assistance on more than a superficial level. It helps us to know what a student thinks about his or her writing; it gives a starting point for instruction. If we value commentary, our own and students', then we need to demonstrate this. Will this significantly reduce our workload or paperwork? Will we read better papers? In addition to a reduction in time spent poring over papers—correcting, editing, and providing unnecessary written feedback—we'll be using our time better and reduce student anxiety and stress. We can begin an ongoing dialogue with students that will be more useful to improve their writing.

Here's how this philosophy can be realistically applied to student writing and integrated in the classroom:

1. *Consider adopting and adapting a portfolio approach for writing.*

    While we won't detail in depth the justification for using a portfolio system in your classroom or school, we encourage you to investigate the literature and research on writing portfolios. Clearly, portfolios, more than storage folders for writing, serve to develop student writers in ways we believe are beneficial. No matter how you adapt a portfolio to meet the needs of your situation, we recommend that it be a flexible tool and always be a work in progress.

2. *Require students to self-assess their writing before submitting it.*

It's essential in practice to demonstrate, repeat, and require that students discuss their own writing. More valuable than concentrating on what they've written, get students to begin writing about how they have written a piece. This dialogue, at first, may be difficult to achieve. With practice and guidance students learn to discuss the mechanics of their writing and their language decisions with insight and more confidence. Encourage them to ask specific questions, for specific suggestions, and admit where they encountered difficulties and ease in their writing. We can't overemphasize the powerful and dramatic impact of this technique on students.

Tip for success: We're not naïve enough to think that every student will embrace this tactic, nor do we think you should expect remarkable changes immediately. This is a gradual process. Student writing must be viewed in a developmental fashion. The technique will affect students intellectually and emotionally. It may crack hard exteriors and result in the kind of writing you have hoped students would produce, and now know they could produce if allowed.

3. *Provide specific written feedback on the piece.*

Teachers have become expert at writing comments to justify low grades or express displeasure with poor writing. We're skilled at praising, too, when we read something deserving accolades. We're not advocating more complicated editing marks or additional canned superficial comments. We've got to provide more substantial types of feedback in writing. Student writers need tangible, straight talk about what they've written and how they've presented it—especially from us. Offering comments judiciously will lead writers to make worthwhile revision.

4. *Respond directly to students' assessment writing.*

Let's not overlook students' notes and personal reflections on a piece of writing. It's an opportunity to respond directly to issues and concerns with concrete answers. Students often ask questions or seek suggestions; again, we've got to determine how much to divulge as a piece develops. The key here is to respond like an interested writer/reader and not so much as a teacher/evaluator.

5. *Focus on major concerns that need attention.*

We must avoid giving more direction than is needed or asked for by students. We shouldn't worry about being inclusive in our remarks and covering everything. Here's a situation in which less is more. Resist the impulse to comment on everything. An incremental approach focused on a principal writing concern works best.

6. *Allow some issues to go unmentioned.*

Some technical and stylistic problems in drafts naturally work themselves out during revision; we can bring attention to these later, once the writing has reached an acceptable form. Too much can happen when we overcorrect details that could quell any further writing development. Writing teachers need to step in at appropriate moments but recognize the need for the student to take responsibility for the draft.

7. *Delay grading a piece until after its agreed-upon final revision.*

While this seems obvious to teachers using a portfolio approach, we must note that students consider a grade on writing as the final point in the process. The reality of school demands that we do eventually grade writing; we're suggesting that this be prolonged as long as possible. Students who only write for a grade quickly learn to give a teacher what she or he wants. Let's not encourage this.

These seven suggestions beg the question: How will this "enlightened" approach affect the traditional type of writing assignments students are required to do in other disciplines or on more formal writing tasks? Will they be able to write within constraints, mandated guidelines, and on demand? Evidence from our classrooms has taught us this:

- Students who are self-assured have power over their abilities, recognize their capabilities and limitations, and work as independent writers.
- They are accustomed to making decisions about purpose, audience, and form.
- They can and do perform well in prescribed situations that don't begin to require the skills they have practiced and developed.
- They might not choose to write within a limited framework, but they can, if asked, write with more success because they've gone through rigorous and intensive training. It's like asking a practiced singer to hum a few bars of a popular tune or an accomplished artist to sketch a picture of a house. It may not be desirable, but they can accomplish the task. The same holds true for our students.

Questioning, Conferencing, and Other Feedback

If we want to be honest with students about their writing and help them progress as far as they can under our tutelage, we've got to continually examine how we interact with them and their texts. Students are resilient and will forgive some misguided advice on our part if we relieve the pressure on them to write perfect papers. When we speak to them about their writing, we must continually get them to make decisions. When we conference with students, we must (1) ask the right questions, (2) get students to reveal honest feelings about their pieces, and (3) offer encouragement in making further decisions. This effort more than anything else we do creates writers out of students.

Here's a short transcribed writing conference with a student illustrating these aims:

KIM: I've got a few questions about the essay due on Wednesday. I know what I want to write about, but I don't know where to go with it.

TEACHER: What are you writing about?

KIM: Well, I'm writing about my grandfather . . . when I used to watch him work in his basement doing carpentry.

TEACHER: What do you want readers to understand after reading your piece?

KIM: I guess I want readers to understand how my feelings about him have changed . . . then and now. When I was a kid, I didn't really appreciate his skill and patience, but I want to write more about how I feel now . . . sort of how I think now about my grandfather. Does that make sense?

TEACHER: Sure. I think your experience *then* is just a way for you to begin writing about what you're thinking now. Do you know what I mean? I wouldn't let the story of your grandfather in the past be the focus, but you might want to start with that. Some readers won't care, so make the focus on your thoughts now. Do you have a few specific points to write about how you feel now?

KIM: I think I do. I mean, now I realize how patient he was, how hard he worked, and how much he cared about doing a good job. Just by watching him I sort of learned all that, but I didn't really know it then. When I think back and then look at my life now, I see that he really taught me a lot.

TEACHER: Then it sounds like that's what you ought to write about.

KIM: So do I write a paragraph about each of those things and give an example of how I saw each quality in him?

TEACHER: I think for a start that would work, see how it plays out when you're writing. Maybe one idea will dominate—so you might want to go with that one for a little longer or maybe a new idea

KIM: And how should I begin this?

TEACHER: Do you have any ideas? Any way to get readers to read this?

KIM: Well, I thought about describing a desk my grandfather made that we have in our den and then kind of going back to talk about him. I don't really know.

TEACHER: That's sounds like good idea. You can always change it later and use this description somewhere else, so it won't be wasted effort. Give it a shot. So, are you ready to go with this?

KIM: Yeah, I think I am.

TEACHER: Just write what you can, and we'll take a look at it later to see what it may need.

This quick conference works well to suggest a direction for a writer. Kim feels better about what she wants to write about and makes many of the choices herself. We can get more specific as the writing progresses.

Here's a written response to a student about a piece at a different stage in its development that gets specific. The response was sent via email and refers to a piece entitled "The Carnage Highway" (see Chapter 6 for the actual excerpt):

Dear Preston,

Here are some of my thoughts on "The Carnage Highway." Hope you get this before class tomorrow.

My Comments:

You've got a lot of honest reflection in this piece. I hear a distinct voice that cares deeply about preserving a pristine place. I was particularly moved by your opening paragraph. The word choices were vivid and powerful. It's an excellent set up for your contrast, later in the piece, between the natural beauty of the Eastern Shore and the cold statistical evidence of building the Interstate highway through this area on both the environment and people. I love the image of "bayside roads meandering through villages." Good stuff!

Suggestions:

I'd like to see you try some sentence combining (I've highlighted spots as possibilities). I'll be doing a mini-lesson on this in class, so you may pick up an idea on this. If possible, I'd like to use a couple of your sentences for a demo. (It may save you some work.) I'd like you to consider your closing. With such a powerful piece, you've got to end BIG! Try a variety of closings to see how they sound. You can share them with your writing group, but you make the final decision. I wonder if you could get back to the natural beauty versus the harsh reality of the highway image with which you began. What would the effect be? I want to talk to you about the balance in this piece—what percentage of the natural environment description you weigh against the highway statistics.

You've got areas to work on here, but I see a strong piece emerging. Play with it a bit and see where it goes.

Hope this helps. Send the revised copy by e-mail, and we'll keep in touch this way. See you in class.

These comments refer to specific choices made by the writer. The general tone is upbeat and practical. The suggestions are just that—suggestions to a writer to consider revisions. It's important to allow writers to make their own decisions, and let them test these revisions with readers. Responding to students in this way is useful for several reasons:

- It guides further instruction.
- It establishes a need for a mini-lesson.
- It asks the writer to consider specific points.
- It establishes a useful dialogue between a reader and a writer.

Tip for success. Teachers don't need to respond in writing to every student draft. That is neither appropriate nor necessary. This is a judgment call on the part of a teacher. This piece had merit, and it warranted written feedback. Knowing when to give this feedback improves with experience, but we always rely on our intuition to decide when and how much. Students will often ask for specific comments. That's a sure sign.

Developing a Personal "Working" Vocabulary

Students have become familiar with the words teachers typically write on their papers and the subjective or objective corrective marks. Students recognize the language and the symbols. Most writing handbooks, many curriculum guides, and many individual schools have agreed on a set of marks to use when responding to student writing. There are several inherent problems with these prescribed/required systems:

- In some cases, students have been anesthetized by these marks.
- The marks are cumbersome to administer and decipher.
- Superficial marks don't promote further deep revision.
- Students don't like to see a lot of edit marks on their papers.

Too often, no matter how carefully we try to administer prescribed marking systems, we've seen the results: students write less and aren't inspired to revise in ways we know they must if they are to develop. So what can we do? If your teaching situation allows, we advocate a simpler and more effective system: a personal system of marks and "working" vocabulary. We suggest that this personal system evolve over time, and that you carefully consider what works and what doesn't—with the idea that if writing is not progressing because of your feedback, then you should reconsider what you're doing.

Provide students with a clear explanation of your marking system. Give them time to become familiar with the terms and marks you use. When students share pieces in writing groups, respond to each other in class, or assess their writing, they can use the same marks and terms. You'll soon develop a community of writers using a language specifically tuned to talk about writing. It's efficient and effective. Here's a student handout explaining ours:

Evaluating Your Writing

Below are the marks that will appear on your drafts. The marks are subject to change and represent one assessment. Many factors influence why these marks appear: tone, feeling, perception, correctness, appropriateness, etc.

These marks are intended to assist you. Use the notations as a starting point; take them for what they're worth and don't let them throw you off the track. Look for these in the margins or underscoring some of your writing.

| This word, phrase, sentence, chunk, section is good; it works. I'm clear about your intent and I have a distinct meaning based on your words. Good writing—a keeper. Do more of this!

|| This word, phrase, sentence, chunk, section is excellent. Your word choice works well; your meaning is clear, interesting, and provoking. This writing jumps off the page. Well done!

☆| Wow ! This word, phrase, sentence, chunk, section is "golden." Impressive word use here. This is special writing—memorable stuff!

{| This word, phrase, sentence, chunk, section needs another look. Work it again; you've got something of merit here but it needs tweaking. Try recasting it.

{ This word, phrase, sentence, chunk, section needs attention. The problems can be superficial or deep structure ones—check it out. Take another look. Consider changing, adding, or deleting. Revise and resubmit.

Occasionally, I use a WC to let you know that you've used a particularly good word. Also, you'll see a ! in the margin, at times, which is exactly what the mark implies anywhere else: an exclamation of surprise.

Here's a sample paper with the marks and terms we employ when we respond to students:

Fear

{ Grade school was a turbulent period of happiness and great sadness. But at the end of it was a turning point; a time of inner struggle for dominance and recognition from a father who expressed love with the back of his hand.

As with most children, we all had an arch rival of some sort, mine went by the name of Billy. Now Billy wasn't just my nemesis, several kids had problems with him. Billy was the type of kid who took your lunch or lunch money, and sometimes just plain beat the snot out of people.

|| A time came when Billy approached me during a recess and took my baseball hat. His taunts flew at me and stung me hard. My face flushed, but I was still composed. Repeatedly I asked for my hat back, only to see it fly back and forth from one hand to another in a game of keep away that ensued for several minutes.

A crowd of onlookers gathered and I could see this was going to father than I wanted it to. Trapped within myself, I waited for the first blow to connect.

It didn't take long as his fists flew in swift movement; blurring before my eyes. Pain exploded in my head as I started the free-fall backward and to the right. I laid there stunned for a moment, then I felt the anger and rage inside me build, flexing its muscles against the bindings I tied them to years ago. I couldn't suppress them any longer and they surged through every limb, gaining strength with every piece of me my demons swallowed and consumed.

Rising to my feet, I asked for my hat again. Trying to remain calm, I stepped closer to Billy, knowing what would happen once I did. His fist balled into a knot of hard flesh as he **WC** sent it flying to head again. His swing never connected as I unleashed the emotions kept dormant for years on Billy.

 I was on the offensive; I threw punches that landed one after another with no intention of stopping. I had him on his heels trying to avoid my blows. I backed him up against a tree, he could not retreat any further. Billy tried to fight back, but I was lost in a sea of hatred. I saw my father standing before me and I punched harder. My fury was loosened and Billy's head bounced off my fist and against the tree trunk again and again.

Soft hands restrained me and Billy fell to the ground unmoving. My teacher wiped the streams of tears from my face and walked me to the principal's office, trying to find out what happened as I told my story between sobs. ||

FIGURE 10–1. "Fear" essay

An Objective/Subjective Balance

Students can and should get credit for formal writing, for meeting deadlines, for self-assessing their work, for sharing in groups, and for working. It's critical to find a balance here. Teachers must determine how to reward effort, process, product—how to place value on both objective aspects of writing and less tangible subjective aspects. Talking with students helps to clarify this issue. It's easy for students to understand that each spelling error they make in writing will count as a five-point deduction, yet more difficult for them to conceive why a paper is average (a C) or above average (a B), but not excellent (an A). The subjective elements we use to make these judgments are baffling to students. They internalize that a grade indicates our feeling about them or their intellect. If we are to assign value to writing in productive ways, we've got to dispel these notions by communicating with students and our evaluation methods.

First, writing teachers must come to terms with this objective/subjective issue. We should clearly delineate our expectations: Do three technical errors in a paper knock it out of contention for being considered acceptable, passing, superior? Are we more concerned about the impact, emotional or intellectual, that a piece of writing has? Will this be valued more than correctness? These are not easy issues to solve or explain to students. They are comfortable with an objective standard, yet they can be stifled by it or irritated by it. They are uncomfortable with a subjective evaluation, and they expect concrete justification for both what's good in their writing and what's not.

What can be done? We can alleviate a good portion of the problem by showing students models for judging a range of writing. Sample student writing can best demonstrate this, but it's best not to use writing of actual students in the current classes. You might save a bank of essays—without names—that reflect the full range. Ensure that students understand the difference between superficial errors (scratches and dents) and more substantial deep structure problems (style and meaning). Students who compose dull, uninviting pieces that are technically correct need a different approach than students who have something exceptional in their writing but lack technical correctness.

Holistic, Incremental, or Intensive Evaluation?
Often what can either promote or inhibit writing beyond the first draft is the type of evaluation that we offer as teachers. We should make students aware of the evaluation spectrum—from holistic to incremental to intensive assessment. Comments should provide useful specific feedback (written and oral) that will encourage further reflection and revision.

Holistic evaluation looks at writing to determine how a piece is working—to ascertain if the work has something worth pursuing. Is the work worth the time it takes to read it? Should the writer pursue the piece?

Incremental evaluation looks at a particular segment of a paper focusing more narrowly on each section. Is the segment clear? Does it work best where it is? What specific revision does it need?

Intensive evaluation examines details of the paper focusing specifically on fine points. Does each section function in the entire paper? Are the mechanics correct? What final revisions are necessary?

Students should have a clear understanding of these three types of evaluation. Writer and reader should communicate expectations for a piece of writing. Decide what evaluation method is appropriate based on these considerations:

- Does the piece have merit?
- At what point in the process is the piece?
- Has the writer asked for specific feedback?
- Will specific revisions be possible?
- Has the writer made a commitment to complete the piece?

Commenting on Student Writing

Teachers value written feedback on student writing and devote a lot of time to writing commentary. Often, we value these comments more than students. We may feel that it's our job to write comments (objective and subjective) and that not to do so would be shirking our responsibility. Students expect comments, and parents, too. We've settled into a routine guided more by perceived expectation than thoughtful consideration. Will students write and benefit from writing if teachers don't respond with comments (good or bad) or a grade? Well, the answer is yes. We know from experience that we cannot ensure that students will write as much as they need to write if we have to (1) comment on every piece, (2) evaluate or correct every piece, or (3) read every piece.

A Realistic Rubric

Most schools have established a set of standards or rubric by course and grade with which teachers evaluate student work. We've seen rubrics that establish minimum competency levels and mastery levels in a variety of categories that we use to judge the abilities of our students. In theory and design, rubrics appear to provide a useful grid with which we can plot achievement or place students. In use, though, a rubric is a scale that limits and labels students. When applied to writing, the rubrics we've seen tend to take a more objective, quantitative stance than subjective and qualitative.

We think it's critical for writing to be judged in many ways. It's possible to design a rubric that sends a clear message to student writers that quality and not only technical correctness is valued and attainable. We offer a sample rubric that you can adapt for your writing classroom. It's critical to develop a working rubric.

WRITING RUBRIC

A
Opening captures and holds readers
Original approach to the topic
Shows depth of thinking
Passionate commitment to the subject
Excellent language choices
Organizational decisions make sense
Writing moves readers intellectually or emotionally
Closing is memorable
Technical aspects are almost flawless

B
Opening captures readers
Thoughtful approach to the topic
Shows depth of thinking
Commitment to the subject evident
Good language choices
Organizational decisions make sense
Writing interests readers
Closing works well
Technical aspects are good

C
Opening interests readers
Thoughtful treatment of the topic
Shows thought but needs more depth
Good word choices
Commitment to the subject evident
Writing is clear
Closing works
Organization needs work
Minor technical deficiencies

D

Opening is not interesting
Uninteresting treatment of topic
Minimal thought evident
Word choices need recasting
No commitment to the subject
Ideas unclear
Organization needs attention
Many technical difficulties

The assumption guiding this particular rubric is that (1) a student has made a reasonable effort and (2) submitted a piece of original writing and (3) this is a final evaluation. Of course, this rubric is easily adapted if the letter grades are nonbinding and the assessment is used as an indicator in the writing process. In either case, students must be aware in advance how the rubric will be applied.

Personalizing Departmental Final Exams

Especially in large schools, teachers who give departmental final exams each year often wish that they could tailor at least a part of the exam to their own classes to suit their own implementation of the curriculum and teaching style. Many times, the structure of a departmental test (typically 60 percent short answer: multiple choice questions on vocabulary words and literary terms, etc. and 40 percent essay on required major works) belies the freedom of choice and student responsibility inherent in a workshop approach.

Following are suggestions for personalizing final exams at all grade levels:

1. *Create an exam where all teachers use the same questions for the first sixty points of the test.* Instead of asking students to recall knowledge, ask them to engage in the processes of reading and/or writing. For example, teachers might use the following configuration and topics:

    Reading and Understanding a Short Story (thirty points): Choose an appropriate story, and have students read the story at the exam site. Ask them short answer questions that focus on comprehension, vocabulary, and analysis/application of literary elements.

    Writing About a Character (thirty points): Give students a general question that complements the curriculum, but which can be responded to in diverse ways.

Directions. Respond to the following topic in a page or two of writing. Write an outline and a rough draft on yellow paper. Organize your thoughts and make any desired revisions and corrections. Write your final copy on white composition paper.

Topic. Suffering from the sorrows of war, poverty, hatred, death, or defeat is a painful experience not only for real people, but for characters from literature as well. Yet, suffering can strengthen an individual's character.

Your writing task. Choose either a character from literature or a person from real life, and show how suffering of some kind made this person stronger. Be sure to accomplish the following:

- Identify the character and related information (book, author, situation, your relationship with the person, etc.).
- Give details about what the person goes/went through and how/why this person deals with suffering.
- Show what the character is like/what he or she has learned/how the character has become stronger as a result of his/her experiences.

FIGURE 10–2. Writing about a character

Figure 10–2 shows a sample appropriate for grades 7–12.

2. Create your own part. Develop an exam where teachers construct the final forty points of the exam to suit their individual classes. This is a viable way for teachers to assess students using methods and topics that are unique to their classes. One of our favorite ways to put together this section is what we call "Just Some Classwork." The teacher chooses twelve or fifteen varied and interesting topics and asks the students to respond to a choice of four. It's a comprehensive way to get students to write for diverse purposes and in many veins: they write as reviewers, evaluators, comics, and academics; as chroniclers, poets, and sages. The following list shows the gamut of what one eighth-grade honors class experienced during a year of English.

Part III: Just Some Classwork (40 points)

Directions: Choose four of the topics/themes listed below, and discuss each topic's meaning, significance to your English education, connection to you personally, and/or connection to our English class.

You will complete this part of your exam in class during workshop and at home. Bring your completed responses to the exam site, where you will hand them in. Your writing will be evaluated for content, organization, style, mechanics, and appearance.

1. The Order of Grammar: Word, Phrase, Clause, Sentence
2. Commas, Semicolons, and Colons
3. Reading Writing Workshop: A Class Act?
4. "The Ants Meet the Boos"
5. Tabloid Truth: Woman Gives Birth to Fully Clothed Baby
6. And the Dicey Goes To . . .
7. The Sod Metaphor
8. Making Judgments About Literature
9. Report and Reflection: Richard Wright's *Black Boy*
10. Literary Technique in Olive Ann Burns' *Cold Sassy Tree*
11. "The Awesome Truth": Paul Zindel
12. The Art of Poetry
13. I Stood at the Shore of the Ocean: A Class Anthology
14. Save What?
15. Free Writing

Tip for success: Because this section of the test is personal by design, some of the topics on this list or any like it will be esoteric. For instance, topic 5 stems from a student who both entertained and irritated classmates all year with his tabloid claims. Topic 6 comes from a student's suggestion based on the class' collective hatred of *Dicey's Song*, the first book they had been required to read the year before: "If we have an Oscar, an Emmy, a Grammy, and a Tony," he exclaimed, "why not give out a fifth award—the Dicey? It could go to the worst book of the year." Topic 14 came about during workshop one day, when students began designing simple posters and slogans and taping them up in the hallways: save the whales, save our sanity, save funky hairstyles, and so on.

Following are the kinds of responses that a "Just Some Classwork" section engenders.

Free writing
MIKE: "What am I supposed to write about? Maybe I'll write about birds with short attention spans who plummet to the earth in the middle of flight. Or virgin amoebas and their first asexual experiences. Deadheads who leach off their parents to buy tickets and follow the Dead around the world. School assignments I never finished? Incorrectly constructed compositions which abruptly end for no reason?"

ALI: "Okay. Free writing time again so I can jot down more . . . kill a limb, chop a tree, consume, consume, consume. Like fire. Or like thick air, the kind that hangs heavy over the sea on August mornings. I love that time. The summer too—my short shorts and rib tops, & walking anywhere I want, and the constant nagging of my age and curfew. Which I don't have. Either."

Making judgments about literature
Note Sandra's suggestions:

"If you write long enough about something you have read, your full judgment will scrub the fungus off your mind and clear your sinuses.

To judge, start to write as soon as you finish reading; the taste of the piece—bright or sweet or ripe or dull—will ring on your tongue. Catch it as it slips off. It is a map of what you have felt.

Reread what you must read. It changes. If it says nothing to your head, search for a part that speaks. Free write about one word or mood or chance you have seen in it. One truth is all you need to see to find how the piece relates to you.

Stray from rules if they bind your fingers. Write your judgments to please no one but yourself, for the truth may speak only to you.

React more. Anything that catches your interest. Songs. Words. Signs. Shoes. Find what it means to you and why and how. The more you use your mind to move your hand, the less rusty and tight the ligaments get, until your thoughts are strong-willed and wise-thinking and loose. It is not enough to love or hate or enjoy or cry about literature. Your paper, your mind, your heart, and hand must all feel it."

Commas, semicolons, and colons
Note this self-conscious piece written in response to a category readers might think students would ignore:

GLENN: "The comma, semicolon, and colon are all necessary tools of writing. One would use a comma to separate items in a list, between the day of the month and the year, following the salutation in a friendly letter, and to separate with a conjunction two main clauses. The semicolon is used to separate related main clauses; however, it can sometimes be used with a conjunction such as "and" or "but" if one of the main clauses has too many commas already. A semicolon can also be used to separate Coram, New York; Duluth, Minnesota; and Paris, Iowa. A colon indicates "note what follows." One uses it to emphasize what he likes to eat: pizza with bacon. Here are other uses of the colon: To Whom It May Concern: and 11:32. Commas, semicolons, and colons provide necessary pauses in writing; therefore, it is important to know how to use them."

Creating Final Portfolio Projects

The "Create Your Own Part" method is a way to integrate traditional testing with portfolio assessment. Teachers can develop a forty-point final portfolio project, like the one that follows, to complement the sixty points on the departmental test.

Teachers who want to create a final portfolio project can do so by reading books and articles on portfolio development and adapting the suggestions and structures they discover with their own ideas. One book we have found helpful is *Portfolios in the Writing Classroom*, edited by Kathleen Blake Yancey (1992); for our project, Roberta Camp's suggestions in "Portfolio Reflections in Middle and Secondary School Classrooms" were fitting.

In general, teachers should devise final portfolio projects that require students to demonstrate the following:

- Presentation folder and table of contents
- A varied and representative sampling of coursework: five to nine pieces
- Both teacher direction and student choice
- Both formal and informal pieces
- Written reflection and assessment of self and growth in relation to both the portfolio and the course

Final Portfolio Project: Seven Plus One

Grade: 7–12 (originally conceived for grade 8; adaptable to all secondary grades)

Time: six to ten class periods

Outcome: Students create final portfolio projects showing samples of their year's work. In reflecting upon their selections, students assess their achievement and growth as readers and writers.

Students should complete a final portfolio project like this one both in school and at home during the last two weeks of regularly scheduled classes.

We begin the project with our classes by distributing and discussing the final project itself (see Figures 10–3 and 10–4):

- We discuss the project thoroughly and answer students' questions:
- We show them both scrap paper (newsprint) and the paper for the portfolio cover itself: 18″ × 18″ ninety-pound-weight white drawing paper, folded into a 12″ × 18″ rectangle—with the flap forming one

Name _____ Date _____

FINAL PORTFOLIO PROJECT: "Seven Plus One"

Each of you will compile and design a portfolio of your year's work:

The "Seven" in the title above refers to the *Seven (7) pieces of writing/work* that you will put into your portfolio.

The "One" in the title refers to Part One of your final exam, a FINAL PORT-FOLIO ASSESSMENT ESSAY that you will write, revise, and rewrite in class and at home. You will receive this Part One question soon, and you will bring both your portfolio and your completed Part One essay to the final exam. With your portfolio, this essay is worth 40% of your exam grade.

PORTFOLIO REQUIREMENTS

Identify and personalize the cover (the folder itself):

1. Design a front cover. Include a title, your name, date, and teacher's name. Consider lettering, illustration, and symbols.

2. Create a "rear end" identification for the back of your portfolio folder—a vanity plate, coat of arms, or logo, etc.

Include a table of contents: Write / design a "Table of Contents" page listing the title of / identification for each of the seven pieces you are including.

(OVER)

FIGURE 10–3. Final portfolio project: seven plus one (1)

long "pocket"—and folded in half again to form a 9″ × 12″ folder with pockets.
*   We show students samples of front and rear covers and offer them a template to use if they choose to design a coat of arms for the rear cover design (Figure 10–5).
*   We demonstrate different ways to design a table of contents, from typed traditionally to designed on the inside cover flap.

Five Pieces of Writing:

1. **Something "Old,"** written in 1997(need not rewrite)

2. **Something "New,"** written and/or finalized in June, 1998

3. **Something Connected to Literature** (may rewrite)
   Ex: A response from your journal, selected and rewritten; a character sketch; a book review; an essay test.

4. **An Important Piece of Writing** (may rewrite)

   Include the piece and your answers to these four questions:

   • Why did you select this particular piece of writing?

   • What was especially important when you were writing this piece?

   • What do you see as the special strengths of this paper?

   • If you continued working on this piece, what would you do?

5. **A Piece Clearly Identifiable as a Type** (need not rewrite) Ex: Explanatory composition, persuasive essay, comparison/contrast, narrative, etc.

Two Pieces of Your Choice: These need not be pieces of writing, but they may be. Choose from among tests and quizzes, projects, journal entries, poems . . . you name it! You might like to choose a piece of writing from an interdisciplinary project or that you originally wrote for social studies class, math class, etc.

Bring all of the portfolio requirements to the final exam.
Important Note:
Put together a portfolio that gives a true picture
Of your writing as it reflects you.
Everything should be honestly and thoughtfully prepared and chosen.
Your portfolio is a collection—a design—of you.
Have fun!

FIGURE 10–4. Final portfolio project: seven plus one (2)

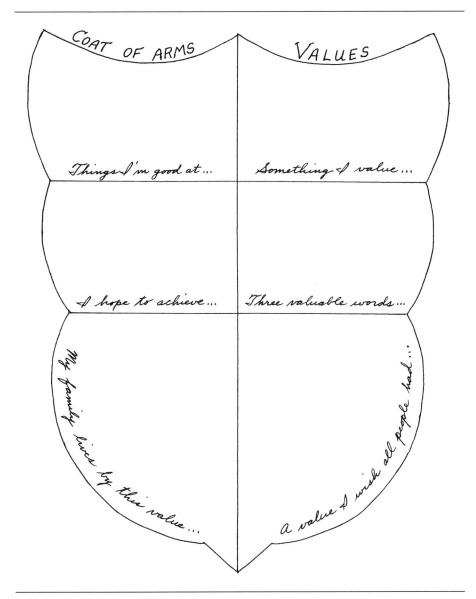

FIGURE 10–5. Coat of arms template

- We give students their writing folders and their working portfolios that contain their year's work so that they can peruse them right away.

A day or two after we've discussed the project, and students have begun to read through their work, make selections, and design coats of arms, we distribute and discuss the "Plus One" part of their assignment, the Final Portfolio Assessment Essay (Figure 10–6).

Note these comments:

- Be sure to distribute and discuss the final assessment requirements along with the project itself. Students need to consider their final

---

English 8   Final Exam

Part One: Final Portfolio Assessment Essay
(40 points, including your portfolio)

Directions: Write a composition of approximately two pages (some students may write more) in which you reflect upon the pieces you have chosen to make up your portfolio. In other words, make some observations and judgments about the writing (and other work) that you have included in your final collection.

Very simply, write a composition about your portfolio.

Consider providing information that answers these questions in your composition:

1. How / why did you choose the pieces you chose?

2. What do you notice about your earlier work? Your recent work? Your work as a whole?

3. How do you think your writing has changed?

4. At what points did you discover something new about writing? What do you now know about writing?

5. In what ways do you think your reading has influenced your writing?

6. How would you rate / evaluate your work this year? Your worth? Your growth?

Note: You will write Part One in class and at home as you compile and prepare your portfolio. Bring your completed portfolio, including your carefully revised, edited, and rewritten Final Portfolio Assessment Essay, to the final exam.

FIGURE 10–6. Final portfolio assessment essay

written assessments while they're compiling and creating portfolios, not after. They have to be able to intertwine all processes involved.

- We designate the "Seven Plus One"—the portfolio and the final assessment essay—as Part I of the test, the part students have to bring to the final exam site. (Another option is to have the portfolio and final assessment essay due a day or two before the exam date.) Parts II and III are the short answer and writing parts of the test, which students take at the exam site itself.

When students complete final portfolio projects, their collections show evidence that they have mastered desired learning standards. Still, as these excerpts from their final assessment essays show, alongside brilliance lies humor and an insistence for growth.

Final Portfolio Project Assessment: A Dozen Student Self-Assessments

1. "I now know that when you write, you should not hold back. If you are thinking something, then write it down, and see how it is."
2. "This year I discovered that writing sometimes helps you find yourself. Kind of like words mean more on paper than they do in your mind."
3. "When I look at my writing from the beginning of the year, I notice that it is not very interesting. Now I find my writing specific and inviting. One thing I learned about writing this year is that you can't think too much. I used to sit and struggle over little things, but now I have learned that if you just write you will enjoy writing a whole lot more."
4. "First of all, my earlier work is rigid. It clearly shows that it was not written openly or freely. It seems to be written with a limit; no personal feeling is shown. My earlier work is also lacking descriptiveness and intelligent words or phrases. It seems to amplify the limited use of my vocabulary. I was not making full use of what I knew."
5. "In my earlier work I wrote essays like I was restating a question. I think last year I was more concerned about proper grammar, but this year I try to make my writing interesting and easier to relate to. I think all the free writing and reading aloud we did in English and social studies helped me learn this. I'm still growing as a writer and reader, but I've really opened up."

6. "The piece entitled 'Me . . . Then and Now' let me finish the story of how I arrived at my present self . . . this piece meant so much to me because this story has been choked back so often, it was time to tell it."

7. "I think that this year science has had a big impact on my writing and reading skills. It has forced me to write almost perfect work and read boring topics for extended periods of time. It has taught me to pay great attention to detail in stories and questions. I had to become very disciplined in this subject, which made my other work rise along with it."

8. "As part of my sampling, I included my 'How to Administer CPR' paper. At first, writing this seemed like it would be a simple task until I realized there are many things taken for granted when giving instructions. If a person has no idea about performing a task, it is necessary to keep things simple, direct, in proper sequence, and to make no assumptions about what the person might already know. I had to rethink this piece of writing a few times before I made it simple enough without omitting life-saving information.

   This piece of writing was surprisingly more difficult that I had originally anticipated. I guess that is why teaching looks easier than it really is."

9. "Aside from the grammar and punctuation getting better, the most noticeable thing about my writing is that I wrote freely. My hand couldn't keep up with my head."

10. "Writing this year has changed me because I used to hate writing poetry, but now I don't care about writing poetry."

11. "I through the course of this year found out that writing is an art."

12. "Writing can't be taught, nor can it be mastered."

Alternative Activity: A Jeopardy Quiz

Grade: 7–12
Time: One class session
Outcome: Encourages using information in a creative way and increases student retention

This activity provides an interesting option for students to demonstrate what they know. It lets them control both questions and answers that lead to strengthening their own learning. Like the popular game show, students provide responses in the form of questions to show what they know. The change in format—writing answers in order to compose questions—breaks the traditional in class quiz routine.

The Jeopardy Quiz lets students practice these valuable skills:

- Focusing on significant information
- Composing good questions
- Collaborating to reach an agreement
- Taking control of their learning

Here are the directions.

Jeopardy Quiz

This activity works well after a reading assignment, class lecture, film, or discussion. On a small sheet of paper, take a few minutes to list important information you've learned and compose a corresponding question for each. Try something like this:

> Answer: We must consider the meaning of rituals.
> Question: What key point is suggested in "The Lottery"?
>
> or
>
> Answer: The neighbor in "Mending Wall" repeats this contradictory idea.
> Questions: What is "Good fences make good neighbors"?

Copy these in your journal or notebook for a record of what you wrote.

Hand in your Jeopardy Quiz answers and questions. I'll create a class quiz using several of the ones you provide. The quiz requires you to supply the questions. You'll have an advantage if I choose your answer and question.

Bonus round

After I return the graded quizzes, you will be able to compare your questions with the actual quiz and with answers/questions of your group. As you compare your notes, consider the following:

> Did you select important information?
> Did you omit information that others in your group recorded?

As a collaborative effort, design a bonus answer/question using a new piece of information that was not on the class quiz. Give your answer to another group and challenge them to provide a correct, corresponding question. This only adds points to your original quiz score. If your group writes a correct question, I'll add the points to your score.

The Jeopardy Quiz helps you develop these useful skills:

- Recognizing important information
- Prioritizing notes/information
- Remembering more of what you read, see, or hear

Special note to teachers: Accept and use a variety of appropriate questions to correspond to the answers. Design a quiz for success. Keep the quiz short and be open to surprises. When you evaluate the responses, it's not necessary to have an exact match. The Jeopardy Quiz adapts a routine activity as a change of pace. You can add information not reflected in what you collect from students, but use mostly student input to design the quiz.

Here's a sample Jeopardy Quiz on Shakespeare's *The Tragedy of Julius Caesar* (Act I and II) that we created with our students' input. We've underlined the key words for each correct response:

1. A: Tribunes, Flavius, and Marullus were angry at Romans for this.
   Q: What is <u>celebrating Caesar's return</u> to Rome?
2. A: He believed that "Men at some times are masters of their fates."
   Q: Who is <u>Cassius</u>?
3. A: Romans "hooted and clapped their chopped hands" at the sight of this three times.
   Q: What is when Mark Antony offered Caesar a <u>crown</u> (and he refused it)?
4. A: Brutus described Caesar as this animal in a shell that must be killed before it's allowed to hatch.
   Q: What is a <u>serpent</u> or snake?
5. A: Caesar's bleeding statue and smiling Romans bathing in its blood.
   Q: What did Calpurnia <u>dream</u> about the night before Caesar's assassination?

BONUS
   A: He was the last conspirator to join the group.
   Q: Who is Cauis <u>Ligarius</u>?

EPILOGUE

We've summarized our final thoughts in the list that follows. This list serves as a starting place for anyone embarking on a teaching career and for veteran teachers desiring change. Our intent is to provoke all teachers to examine systematically what they do.

We suggest that all teachers who want to engage their students and make learning meaningful and fun design lessons incorporating these tenets:

1. Connection to the World: Find ways to connect content in the classroom to real-world situations. Demonstrations and simulations work well.
2. Student Voice: Allow students to express themselves in diverse and constructive ways. Consider alternatives to traditional study and presentation methods.
3. Freedom: Provide opportunities for choice within structure. Reduce prescriptive directions so that students must make choices and take on responsibility. They'll learn to make good decisions.
4. Pursuit of Genuine Interest: Create interest in exploration of the unknown. Present students with a diverse menu of possibilities and let them find their way.
5. Room for the Truth: Encourage honest inquiry in all areas of study. Allow for discussion that gets to core of the issues and answers questions. Push students to the highest level possible.
6. Authentic Assessment: Use common sense in evaluating student work. Provide every means for success and reward growth.

We challenge teachers to make their lessons exciting for students by promoting curiosity and maintaining high expectations. Develop an urgency about the time spent in a classroom; make it vital. All the best.

BIBLIOGRAPHY

Alley, Rick. 1997. "Tomato." *The Talking Book of July: Poems*. Spokane: Eastern Washington University Press.

Atwell, Nancie. 1997. *In the Middle*. Portsmouth, NH: Boynton/Cook.

Bloom, Benjamin. 1994. *Bloom's Taxonomy: A Forty-Year Retrospective: Ninety-Third Yearbook of the National Society for the Study of Education, Part 2*. Chicago: University of Chicago Press.

Bly, Carol. 1992. "Talk of Heroes." *The Tomcat's Wife and Other Stories*. New York: Harper Perennial Library.

Britton, James. 1982. *Prospect and Retrospect: Selected Essays*. Portsmouth, NH: Boynton/Cook.

Burns, Olive Ann. 1984. *Cold Sassy Tree*. New York: Ticknor & Fields.

Camp, Roberta. 1992. "Portfolio Reflections in Middle and Secondary School Classrooms." In *Portfolios in the Writing Classroom*, edited by Kathleen Blake Yancey. Urbana, IL: National Council of Teachers of English.

Cherry, Lynne. 1992. *A River Ran Wild*. New York: Harcourt Brace.

Cisneros, Sandra. 1984. *The House on Mango Street*. NY: Random House, Inc.

Clark, William M. 1972. "The Supermen." In *Playboy's Short-Shorts 2*. Chicago: Playboy Press.

Daniels, Harvey. 1994. *Literature Circles: Voice and Choice in the Student-Centered Classroom*. Markham, Ontario: Pembroke Publishers.

Dickinson, Emily. 2001. "Tell All the Truth but Tell It Slant." In *Literature: An Introduction to Reading and Writing*, 6th ed., edited by Edgar V. Roberts and Henry E. Jacobs. Upper Saddle River, NJ: Prentice Hall.

Emerson, Ralph Waldo. 2000. *The Essential Writings of Ralph Waldo Emerson*. Princeton, NJ: Princeton Review.

Ferlinghetti, Lawrence. 1974. "Autobiography." *A Coney Island of the Mind: Poems*. New York: W. W. Norton.

Fortunato-Galt, Margot. 1992. *The Story in History: Writing Your Way into the American Experience*. New York: Teachers and Writers Collaborative.

Frost, Robert. 2001. "Mending Wall." In *Literature: An Introduction to Reading and Writing*, 6th ed., edited by Edgar V. Roberts and Henry E. Jacobs. Upper Saddle River, NJ: Prentice Hall.

Gibran, Kahlil. 1997. *The Prophet*. Ware, Hertfordshire: Wordsworth Editions Ltd.

Golding, William. 1959. *Lord of the Flies*. New York: Prentice Hall.

Holt, John. 1995. *How Children Fail*. New York: Perseus.

Hunt, Irene. 1987. *Across Five Aprils*. New York: Berkley Publishing Group.

Jackson, Shirley. 2001 "The Lottery." In *Literature: An Introduction to Reading and Writing*, 6th ed., edited by Edgar V. Roberts and Henry E. Jacobs. Upper Saddle River, NJ: Prentice Hall.

Johnson, D. W., et al. 1991. In *Cooperation in the Classroom*. Edina, MN: Interaction Book Company.

Jones, Seaborn. 1996. "The Red Horse." *Lost Keys*. Valdosta, GA: Snake Nation Press.

Knowles, John. 1985. *A Separate Peace*. New York: Prentice Hall.

Lee, Harper. 1998. *To Kill a Mockingbird*. New York: Little Brown.

Macrorie, Ken. 1984. *Writing to Be Read*. Portsmouth, NH: Boynton/Cook.

———. 1988. *The I-Search Paper*. Portsmouth, NH: Boynton/Cook.

Miller, Arthur. 1987. *A View from the Bridge: A Play in Two Acts with a New Introduction*. New York: Viking Press/Penguin Plays.

———. 2001. *Death of a Salesman*. In *Literature: Reading, Reacting, Writing*, 4th ed., edited by Laurie G. Kirszner and Stephen R. Mandell. Forth Worth: Harcourt College Publishers.

Moffett, James. 1992. *Active Voice: A Writing Program Across the Curriculum*. Portsmouth, NH: Boynton/Cook.

Orwell, George. 1968. "Politics and the English Language." In *Collected Essays, Journalism and Letters of George Orwell*, edited by Richard Johnson. New York: Grolier.

———. 1990. *1984*. New York: New American Library Classics.

Orwell, George. 1996. *Animal Farm*. Upper Saddle River, NJ: Prentice Hall.

Rosenblatt, Louise M. 1996. *Literature as Exploration*. 5th ed. New York: Modern Language Association.

Rylant, Cynthia. 1993. *Appalachia*. New York: Trumpet Club.

Salinger, J. D. 1951. *The Catcher in the Rye*. New York: Little Brown.

Shakespeare, William. 1992. *The Tragedy of Julius Caesar*. New York: Washington Square Press.

————. 2000. *The Tragedy of Macbeth*. New York: Washington Square Press.

Steinbeck, John. 1993. *Of Mice and Men*. New York: Penguin Books.

————. 2000. *The Pearl*. New York: Penguin Books.

Taylor, Mildred. 1997. *Roll of Thunder, Hear My Cry*. London: Puffin.

Tsujimoto, Joseph I. 1988. *Teaching Poetry Writing to Adolescents*. Urbana, IL: National Council of Teachers of English.

Voigt, Cynthia. 2002. *Dicey's Song*. New York: Pocket Books.

Vygotsky, Lev. 1986. *Thought and Language*, edited by Alex Kozulin. Cambridge, MA: MIT Press.

Whitman, Walt. 1993. "I Hear America Singing." In *A Treasury of Great Poems*. New York: Simon & Schuster.

Williams, Tennessee. 2001. *The Glass Menagerie*. In *Literature: Reading, Reacting, Writing*, 4th ed., edited by Laurie G. Kirszner and Stephen R. Mandell. Forth Worth: Harcourt College.

Wood, George H. 1993. *Schools That Work*. New York: Plume.

Wright, Richard. 1998. *Black Boy*. New York: Prentice Hall.

INDEX

Writing about place, 100–02
Writing conferences, 164–66
Writing needs assessment, 16–17
Writing to Be Read, 65

Y
Yancey, Kathleen Blake, 176